FIGHTING F

Books By   JJ Williams

Living with depression, My depression journal, Volume 1

Living with depression, My depression journal, Volume 2

Living with depression, My depression journal, Volume 3

Psych Ward, True story of mental health

Twisted Rose

Deadly Affair

Love Hurts

FIGHTING FOR MY LIFE

JJ WILLIAMS

Dedicated to anyone who has ever suffered from depression, has abused alcohol, has felt like no one has ever cared about you, and has been betrayed by the people who were supposed to love you the most.

Do not give up! Better days can come for you.

FORWARD

By   S.F.

I have had a case manager / client relationship with Jason for many years now, and I feel Blessed that I was asked to write this. As a case manager for over ten years, I have seen many clients fight their way out of dark places to a place of stability and happiness. When I applied for a case manager position all those years ago, I had no idea what I was getting myself into, but I would not change it for the world. Jason is one of those reasons why. My first meeting with Jason was in a group setting where he was extremely quiet and refused to do "homework" or paperwork of any kind. Fast forward a year or so, and Jason needed a new case manager. At that time, I honestly could not take on any more clients, but Jason was requesting me only as his new case manager. I agreed to work with Jason as I was invested not only in my job, but Jason as a client. Jason came back to the group, and he decided to really put some effort into it. Jason started participating a lot more, filling out his paperwork, and putting other people in their place when they weren't taking the group seriously.

Every day I see people struggle, and that is what motivates me to continue doing what I do. Jason has had his struggles along the way, but he has come a long way since he started working on his mental health. Jason went from staying in a homeless shelter to a group home to a sober living facility. Jason then found independent living on his own. Jason finally found some peace in his life, and he started writing, and telling his stories.

I am very happy for Jason. I know he used to hate reading and writing. Now, he has made himself successful by doing it. Jason is always thinking about ways to better himself, and I am always the first person he shares his ideas with.

I am glad that I am one of the only people Jason says he trusts. I often tell other clients about Jason's idea of writing and publishing his depression stories. Jason is definitely inspiring other people.

Way to go Jason!

THE BEGINNING

I have changed my mind. I do not want to die!

Since I plan on sticking around for a while longer, I have a story to tell you. I am going to start at the beginning. I am going to tell you the truth, the whole truth, and nothing but the truth. Telling the truth is very important to me because, from what I have experienced, not many people tell the truth these days.

So, here is my story.

I was born in Tiffin, Ohio, on August 6th, 1974. Tiffin is a small town, and it wasn't so bad when I was younger, but it changed a lot over the years. Places change with the times, I guess. I don't think Tiffin changed for the better though. There are no stores left in Tiffin for shopping, except for Walmart. There used to be a lot more to do here, but a lot of things have closed down over the years. I guess that's why a lot of people spend their time in the bars drinking because Tiffin has plenty of bars for being a small town.

I grew up in a mobile home park. We lived in one mobile home park until I was five years old, then we moved our trailer about two hundred yards away to a different mobile home park. We lived across the street from the fairgrounds. We basically just moved from the south side of the fairgrounds to the north side.

I never thought much about living in a trailer when I was younger, but I felt embarrassed about it when I got a little older because our house looked trashy compared to some of my friend's houses. We didn't have as much money as a lot of other families did.

My mom and dad divorced when I was three years old. I can remember some things from when I was that young, but I don't remember my mom and dad ever living together. I only remember a couple of times with my dad at that early age.

One time I remember it was breakfast time at his house, my brother and I were being loud or something, and we were getting yelled at by my dad. I don't remember anything else about that time.

Another time I remember was being at a bar with my dad. My brother and I were running around, playing around the pool table, and playing songs on the jukebox. I can't recall my thoughts from that far back, but I am sure that was fun for toddlers our age.

Those two times are all I can remember being with my dad. For all I know, those two times could have been back-to-back in the same weekend. Friday at the bar, and then breakfast on Saturday morning.

I do remember times when my brother Nick and I were waiting for my dad to come get us for the weekend, but he didn't show up.

The next memory I have of seeing my dad was a few years later, but I was still very young. My aunt Julie took my brother and I with her when she went to visit him in prison. The only thing I remember about that trip is goofing around on the car ride there with my brother, and my cousin Jim. We always had fun when the three of us were together. That trip to see my dad in prison was the last time I saw him until I was like sixteen years old.

There is something that I didn't know until recently. I was told by my uncle that when my brother and I were very young, my dad had a habit of dropping us off at my grandma's house, and then he would take off for a few days. That really got to me when I heard that. I guess it's true. I don't know why someone would randomly tell me something like that from forty-seven years ago. From what I know now, it doesn't surprise me at all.

Something else I can remember is, I told my mom that I wanted a Cincinnati Bengals coat for Christmas one year. I remember that, but it doesn't make any sense to me. I never liked the Bengals. I guess I was influenced by a neighborhood kid.

When I told my mom about wanting the coat, she told me to write a letter, and send it to my dad, so I did that. I don't know what happened. Either my mom didn't really send the letter, or my dad just didn't want to get the coat for me. I don't know why he wouldn't get it for me if my dad did get the letter I wrote, he surely didn't get me anything else. Actually, I can't remember my dad ever getting anything for me when I was a kid, or ever in my life. I don't know because I never thought to ask, but maybe my dad never wanted kids, so he never wanted to see us or do anything for us.

I was very young when I first got interested in football. I have seriously been a Pittsburgh Steelers fan for forty-five years. When I was like five, the Steelers were the first team that I ever heard of. It was towards the end of the great years they had in the 1970s. Actually, most of the kids in my neighborhood liked the Steelers. I learned a lot about them at a young age, mostly from John Smith and Glenn Weible. They were both a couple of years older than me, so they both knew a lot more about the Steelers to teach me. I quickly learned a lot about them, and the Steelers have always been a big part of my life. It is rare to see me without wearing a Steelers hat or shirt to this day.

Another one of my first memories from when I was very young is the Beatles. My brother Nick and I were climbing around in our hallway closet, and we found a couple of Beatles records on the top shelf. At first, we just played around with the records, but when we were taught to play them the right way, we discovered some music that we liked. The albums we found were Magical Mystery Tour, and Sgt. Pepper's Lonely Hearts Club Band. We didn't know it at that time, but they were classics, and possibly two of the greatest of all time. Sgt. Pepper's is the best album ever in my opinion.

My next discovery of music at an early age was Queen and Kiss. A couple of brothers who lived down the street from us named Tony and Jimmy had records of those two bands, and I listened to them at their house. I instantly liked them both.

Still to this day, Queen and the Beatles are my favorite bands. I still listen to them regularly. Music has always been a very important part of my life. I don't listen to Kiss as much anymore. As I got older, I realized that they got their reputation because of the way they looked, not because of their music.

I wasn't even five years old when I discovered some great music. My love for music just grew and grew after that.

I wasn't even four years old until August in 1978, but I remember the blizzard in 1978. It was so cold, and the snow was piled up all around our mobile home. We made tunnels in the snow, and we crawled around in them around our trailer. That was fun.

Also in 1978, my mom got married for a second time. I guess she didn't waste any time moving forward. My first memory of Mark was, I can't remember the year, but we were visiting him in prison. I guess my mom liked guys that were into getting into trouble and going to prison.

I remember that day visiting Mark in prison, and he was acting like everything was going to be okay. I guess he was a good actor because I had no clue that nothing was going to be okay.

My next memories of my new stepdad were all horrible. At a young age, I am sure that I wasn't doing anything wrong other than normal little kid stuff, but my stepdad was abusing me every day. I don't quite remember, but I am sure it was for things like being a loud kid, or not cleaning my room good enough. I just remember that I was always in trouble and being abused. I had an imaginary friend when I was a little kid. His name was Roggy. When I was in trouble a lot when I was a kid, I tried to blame Roggy so I wouldn't get into trouble. Blaming him never worked out for me though. I always tried my best though.

There were a lot of times when I was in trouble, I had to stand up with my arms straight out forward with a flat baking sheet across my arms, and my stepdad stacked up books or something heavy on the baking sheet, so it was heavy for me. I was a small child, and it didn't take much to be too heavy for me. When my arms got tired, and I dropped the books, I had to start over. I was forced to do that a lot. I hated that. I seriously felt like my stepdad was torturing me. It wasn't very pleasant, and I know that I didn't do anything to deserve that.

I remember my stepdad always saying to me, you are going to be grounded until you are eighteen. He may have said that in a joking way, but it was basically true. I was grounded for most of my first eighteen years. I didn't get to do much as a child.

There were a lot of times when I was a child, my stepdad would yell for me when I was in my bedroom just to get his cigarettes or the TV remote control for him. I always thought that was so stupid. I was three rooms away, but he called for me to do stuff for him. He was a lot closer than I was. He was only a few feet away from what he usually wanted, but I guess he was too lazy to move that far to do something for himself. I was an innocent child, not a damn slave.

I was in the first grade twice. My grades weren't that bad at that age, but I missed too many days of school during my first year of first grade. I didn't miss any days from being ill, I missed too many days of school from having too many bruises on me from being abused by my stepdad.

My teacher asked me a few times if everything was okay at home since I missed so much school, but I always said yes. I should have told her the truth, but I was scared. I learned to not say anything to anyone. I knew sometimes when I talked at home, I would get abused. So, I didn't say much to anyone else either. I was scared that my stepdad would find out that I said something, and I would get beat on more than I already was getting. I knew I didn't want that so I always kept my mouth shut when I wasn't sure if I should say anything.

We lived about a mile away from where I went to grade school. I was only allowed thirty minutes to walk home from school. I don't know what anyone else thinks, but it wasn't always easy for a seven-year-old to walk that far with a time limit. When I didn't make it home by three thirty, I got abused when I got home. Most days I remember walking home as fast as I could so I wouldn't be late.

One day during my second year of first grade, I didn't care about being late, and getting into trouble. I just wanted to act like a kid and do what all the other kids were doing.

After school one day, I went over to my friend, Matt Newland's house. He lived halfway between the school and my house. I had a lot of fun hanging out with Matt. I paid for it when I got home though. I didn't get home until around five o'clock. I was an hour and a half late. I got beaten so badly that day. I couldn't say anything, or it would 've been worse for me, so I couldn't do anything but except it. I tried harder to never be late again after that. It really wasn't worth it to try and act like a kid, I guess.

I tried everything I could to be away from home, and act like a kid without getting into any trouble. I went to CCD classes when I was a kid. CCD was a Catholic school class. I didn't go to a Catholic school, but I went to Catholic school classes. I wasn't into religion when I was younger. The only time I went to church was when I stayed at my grandma Williams house for the weekend, and I went to church with her. I wasn't interested in going to church. I usually just played around on the kneeling benches. My grandma didn't appreciate that very much. She was serious about going to church.

After a while of going to CCD classes, I didn't want to go anymore. I definitely didn't tell my mom though. So, after school, instead of going to CCD on Wednesday's, I started going to my friend Jason Kear's house. He lived right by St. Mary's church, and school. It was always fun going to Jason's house. I was able to feel free and be a kid. I wasn't getting into any trouble either because my mom thought that I was at CCD.

I did everything I could think of to be away from home. My friend, Shawn, talked me into joining Cub Scouts, and I thought that was a great idea. I don't know how I was allowed to do that, but it happened.

I liked Cub Scouts, and the meetings were at Shawn's house, so I just saw that as an excuse to be away from home. I had fun because there were other friends of mine from school there.

In 1979, my half-sister was born. I remember telling my mom that I didn't want a sister, and I wanted to move out of the house when she came. I was five years old, so I guess I wasn't very serious about that, but everyone thought it was funny when I said that.

I was used to it being just my brother and me. I didn't want a girl around. Looking back now, I believe I was right. She is nothing more than a drama filled drug dealer. I will move on because I don't have anything good to say about her.

My happiest times during my early years were being at my grandpa and grandma May's house. I spent a lot of weekends with them on their farm. My grandpa was my favorite person in the world. I thought everything he did was cool. I even thought that I was cool when I was just a little kid, and my grandpa gave me sips of his beer. I didn't like the taste of beer back then, but I liked it just because my grandpa liked it. I got into fishing when I was very young because my grandpa liked to fish, and he taught me how.

I always loved riding on the tractor with my grandpa on the farm. He let me turn the steering wheel sometimes, and I felt like I was seriously doing something important.

My grandpa was only angry with me one time during my life, and I don't blame him. He wasn't mad at me for long because he couldn't stay mad at me.

I was twelve and my brother was thirteen when we started smoking cigarettes. My brother started first, and I guess I followed him. We were smoking once out in the barn at my grandpa's house, and I flicked the cigarette down when I was finished with it. That was a bad idea. I caught the hay, and the barn on fire. My grandpa wasn't very happy about that.

During that time, my mom and stepdad knew that we smoked. They said they would allow it, but it had to be supervised. They knew if they didn't allow it, we would just do it behind their backs.

The reason they found out about us smoking was, my brother got caught for shoplifting a pack of cigarettes. We were at home one day, and the phone rang. It was someone from the police station. My stepdad said they had to go get my brother, and I was told to stay at home, and wait for my sister to get home from Brownies. Brownies were something like Girl Scouts. I knew we were going to be in trouble, and some abuse was coming. As soon as they left to go pick up my brother, I was gone, I ran away.

I can still picture that day. I was wearing my green Drummond Island, Michigan T-shirt, tan shorts, and old beat-up shoes. It was raining outside, but I knew I had to leave.

I had to go somewhere where I knew I would feel safe. Melmore is about eight miles from Tiffin, but I ran to my grandma Williams house. I was getting soaked from the rain, but I knew I had to get there. I can't recall how long it took me, but I made it most of the way on my own. I was twelve years old, and I was afraid of what was coming. I knew since my brother got caught, they would find out that I was smoking also. I had that day off from the abuse, and I wanted to keep it that way.

Melmore is a very small town. I made it all the way to the Melmore school when someone pulled up beside me. I recognized the voice that said, Jason, what are you doing? Get in here. It was my uncle Joe and aunt Joan. They were on the way to my grandma's house, and they picked me up.

I just remember saying, I am going to grandma's house. When I got to my grandma's house, everyone was there. Grandma, grandpa, aunts, uncles, and cousins. That was normal at my grandma's house when I was young. She had ten children.

I felt safe when I got there. I don't remember exactly what I said to anyone, or why I was there unexpectedly. I am sure I said something though, but not too much. There was a lot I never told anyone about what was going on at home. I am sure some people in my family knew something was going on though. There is something I didn't know until recently. I was talking to my aunt, and she told me that child services were called on my mom a few times when I was younger, but nothing ever happened.

I was happy to see everyone when I arrived at my grandma's house, but she immediately called my mom, and they came to get me. On the ride home, I was asked why I left since I was supposed to stay at home and wait for my sister to get home. I just said that I wanted to visit my grandma. I didn't know what else to say, and I didn't want to say too much.

Maybe they were worried that I told everyone about the way I got treated at home because I got grounded on top of the grounding I was already serving, but I didn't get abused when I got home. Actually, it never came up again.

After that, my brother and I were allowed to smoke with supervision. I am sure it would have been a lot worse for me that day if I hadn't run to my grandma's house. I believe it helped me a lot by doing that. I just knew how bad things usually were for me, so I felt that I needed to do something to protect myself.

I spent a lot of weekends at my grandma Williams house when I was younger also. It was always so much fun there. I liked hanging out with my uncle Ben, uncle Dave, and aunt Virginia. They were the youngest of my grandma's children, so they were still around when I was there all the time.

A lot of times when I was at my grandmas for the weekend, my cousin Jim was there also. When my brother, my cousin Jim, and I were together, we were like the three stooges. We were always being goofy. I remember one time we wanted to make some money. We made a sign, and we stood out by the road trying to get the cars to stop. We thought we were acrobats, and we were going to charge people to see us rolling down the hill. No cars stopped, and we didn't make any money though. It was a lot of fun though. My cousin Jim passed away when he was in his early twenties, and I still think about him a lot. I still miss him.

My best friend during my grade school years was Kent Reinbolt. Usually when I was allowed to do anything with friends, I hung out with him at his house. He lived close to us. Kent lived in the mobile home park we lived in before we moved when I was five years old.

Other than hanging out with Kent, when I was allowed to go out and be a kid, I always played in the field down our street. We had some serious football games on that field. That is where I learned how to be athletic.

John Smith really taught me how to play. In the beginning I fumbled the ball a lot every time I got hit. John taught me how to hold on to the ball better. Ryan Smith was his brother, we were friends, but I think Ryan always wanted to hit me hard and hurt me.

I was the smallest kid in my neighborhood, so I had to become very fast so I wouldn't take the hard hits from the bigger kid's. It worked out for me. I became very fast.

I have always been an animal lover. My first cat I ever had was when I was younger. He was a grey cat named Smoky. He was my best buddy when I was little. After a while, he got more interested in being outside, but he still came home to eat every day. The population of cats grew with Smoky being outside. He got every female cat in our neighborhood pregnant.

The first dog I had was named Gizmo. He was a loveable fuzzy ball of fur. Gizmo was always by my side when I was at home. He would never go near my stepdad. I guess even my dog was afraid after witnessing the abuse I went through. I have always loved pets. They are very loyal.

My life didn't start off very well. It definitely wasn't very fun, and I wasn't a happy child. My family didn't have much, and I never had anything too nice. I can't recall anything I ever had as a child that made me extremely happy. The best things that I did receive didn't come from my mom or dad, they came from my grandma and grandpa May. They always got me from favorite things as a child. My grandpa always spoiled me when he saw me.

The only thing I ever received from my dad was a pellet gun. I am not sure that was the best gift for a toddler. I am not a big fan of guns, and I will get into more about that later.

Things were not going well for me, but I was hoping things would get better since I was starting Jr high school soon, but not so fast.

One more horrible thing happened to me when I was thirteen. Something that definitely changed my life forever. It was something that I never talked about until recently when I started writing and telling my stories. I promise, this is the last time I will ever bring it up again. It is something I have been trying to forget for years.

THAT'S GOING TO LEAVE A SCAR

In the summer of 1987, I was preparing to start Jr high school at the end of August. I was a bit nervous about it. I was doing okay in school, but I wasn't a great student. I didn't know how I would do once I started having to change classrooms for every class. That was my main focus at the time.

My stepdad's brother Clifford was living with us at the time. It was already crowded at our house. We originally had a two-bedroom mobile home, but we recently added another bedroom. So, we had three bedrooms, five people, plus another one now.

Clifford was one of those kinds of people who never worked. He just stayed with anyone who would take him. I remember when he showed up at our house, he was bleeding, and his hand and arm were all cut up. He said that he was attacked by a random person.

A couple of days later, my stepdad's sister called, and said her house was broken into, and all of her electronics were stolen. Well, it wasn't very difficult to put two and two together. Clifford used his hand to break the window, and that explained how he cut his hand and arm. He was a thief. He proved that he would even steal from his own sister.

I think it was about six months, but I'm not sure that Clifford was living with us. We always got along until he did what he did. I just overlooked it when he made jokes about me always getting yelled at and abused at home. Sometimes it sounded like he was giving me advice so I wouldn't get in trouble so much, but I wasn't sure. Maybe he was just an arrogant asshole.

One day Clifford told me a joke that was very funny. After he told me the joke, I laughed, and I just went on my way.

Later on, that same day, I couldn't remember the joke, so I asked him to tell it to me again so I could repeat it to someone else. Clifford said he would tell the joke to me again later. He wasn't doing anything else at that time, but I just said, okay.

Later that night it was time, so I just went to bed. I don't know how long I slept, but I got woken up by Clifford. He said, "I will tell you the joke now. I was still half asleep, but I said, okay.

I was asleep on the top bunk of our bunk beds, and he told me to come down to the bottom bunk, and he would tell me the joke again. I climbed down, and I sat on the side of the bottom bed.

Clifford told me to lay down beside him. I laid down, and he told me the joke again. Afterwards I laughed again, but when I rolled over to get up and back up to the top bunk, he told me to stay on the bed. Clifford held my arm so I couldn't move. Then he started touching my leg, he put his hand in my shorts, and he started touching me.

I think I was in shock or something. I'm not sure exactly. I was so scared. I just started crying. He didn't touch me very long because I started crying too loud. He told me to be quiet, so I didn't wake anyone else up. I got up, and I got back onto the top bunk. I continued to cry quietly.

I knew I didn't want to wake anyone else up. I knew I probably would have gotten in trouble for it. I don't know how long it was, but I finally went back to sleep. I guess our reasons for me to be quiet that night were different reasons. I didn't want to get myself in trouble, but he didn't want himself to get into any trouble.

When I woke up the next morning, Clifford and all of his stuff was gone. He didn't have much of anything anyway, but it was all gone. I overheard my stepdad say, Clifford was gone that morning before anyone else woke up. He said that was strange that he didn't even say goodbye.

I didn't say a word. I was afraid I would be in trouble if I said something. I just knew that what happened the night before wasn't right.

The next few days I had a lot of thoughts running through my mind about what had happened. I was only thirteen at that time, so my thoughts probably weren't accurate. I was wondering if I should say something to my stepdad. I was wondering if that made me a bad kid. I was wondering if that meant that I was gay. I really didn't know what to think.

Finally, a few days later, we were at the Red Horse bar eating. We never went anywhere nice to eat, we always went to a bar so my stepdad could drink beer. While we were there, my stepdad said something about Clifford leaving. Finally, I knew I had to say something, but I was scared. So, I said, I don't want to be in trouble, but I know why Clifford left. My stepdad said, "How do you know?

So, I had to say it. I said, he touched my private parts the other night. My stepdad said, "What are you talking about.

I said, he held me down, he put his hand in my shorts, and he touched me.

Well, I didn't get in trouble for saying anything. Actually, he didn't have much of a reaction. He had his money lying on the table, he picked it up, and he gave me four dollars. I guess he thought that was supposed to make everything right.

After that, no one in my family ever brought it up again. It bothered me for many years. Every time it popped into my mind, I quickly tried to think of something else to make it go away.

The bad part is that my mom and stepdad never confronted him about it. They never went to the police about it. They never did anything about it to protect me from it. That is very sickening if you ask me. The adults in charge didn't do anything to protect a child from something like that. If you ask me, my stepdad is as responsible as his brother since he didn't do anything about it.

This experience really changed me. I for sure wasn't the same after that anymore. I didn't trust anyone, and I had a bad attitude towards a lot of things and people. I hated my mom and stepdad after that. I learned at a young age, if I couldn't trust my family, who could I trust? I felt like I was alone from that moment on.

There was a time in 2007 when my stepdad was bullying me about something, and I threw that in his face. He was trying to make me out to be the bad guy about something like he always did, so I said, I was never the problem, it has always been you. I asked him after all those years, why didn't you do anything about what your brother did to me? He just had a dumb look on his face, and he didn't say anything.

I only saw Clifford one more time after he did what he did to me. I just walked away when I saw him, but really, I wanted to beat the shit out of him. I wanted to destroy him like he did me. I am glad I didn't do that though. He really wasn't worth it. He wasn't worth me getting myself into trouble for it. I didn't need any kind of trouble at that point in my life.

I was already nervous about starting Jr high school soon, and this didn't help me any by happening a few weeks before school started.

EVERYTHING WENT TO HELL

I got into Jr high school, and I was instantly lost. Not only did I have a schedule of classes to figure out now, but friends also weren't the same as they were just three months ago in grade school. Everyone was going in different directions. I knew immediately that it wasn't going to be easy for me. I had a lot of classes with Kent, we were still friends, but he was even heading in a new direction. I needed to find myself, I guess.

I loved the 1980's, and my favorite style was long hair, torn jeans, and rock band t-shirts. So, that is what I went with during that time. I guess it worked for me since it wasn't a nice style, and we didn't have much money so I could buy nicer clothes anyway. I did like that style, but it was also a lack of options.

I always wore a hat when I could, but I couldn't wear a hat during school. I looked horrible with long hair. I stuck with it for a few years.

I was lost during those years. I was very quiet and shy. I didn't really say much to anyone. Maybe it was because of what happened to me during the summer before I started Jr high school. I didn't really fit in anywhere. Sometimes I hung out with the long hair rocker kids, sometimes I hung out with the country boy kids, and sometimes I hung out with the good crowd that my long-time friend Kent was in. It was a strange time for me.

I started to notice girls during this time also. I still remember the first girl I liked in seventh grade. Her name was Jill. I was always too shy to talk directly to her, so I always had a friend say stuff to her for me. She always said, no. It was probably for the best. I would have been too shy to talk to her face to face anyway if we did spend time together. I didn't have any confidence back then.

There were two girls I noticed that I was instantly terrified of when I started seventh grade because they were the most beautiful, and they seemed so perfect. I told them both years later that I was terrified of them, they both laughed, and asked me why. I saw Tosha and Mindy as the best girls when I started Jr high school. I guess I was just embarrassed because my clothes weren't very nice. They were cheap since that is all we could afford.

I stopped doing my paper route when I was in Jr high school. I wasn't earning any money by doing it anyway. My stepdad always stole the money when I collected it from the customers. Most of the time I didn't even have the right amount of money to turn into the paper company. I am sure that they always wondered why the money was short, but they never said anything.

I was allowed to go roller skating sometimes when I was in Jr high school. I had a little more freedom during that time. Kent got me into going roller skating, so I went with him when I was allowed to go. I wasn't very good at first, but I got better the more I went. A lot of friends I knew always went skating. It was the cool thing to do back then.

Basketball wasn't my favorite sport to play, but I played basketball when I was in the eighth grade. I was a good basketball player, but I didn't play a lot that year. I was shorter and built smaller than other kids. I played behind Kent and Ron that year. They were both taller than me. They were both good friends though. I got caught smoking in the alley by the school by the ninth-grade basketball coach, so I was suspended for one of our basketball games. I didn't really fit in on the team anyway. I definitely looked out of place in our team picture since I was the only player with long hair, and shoes that didn't match our uniform. I liked being away from home, so I think that is why I played basketball that year. My mom and stepdad never went to any of my games. That didn't surprise me though. It was obvious that they never cared about me.

I got into bowling during my Jr high school years. I picked up bowling very quickly, and I became a very good bowler. That is when I became good friends with Ron because he joined my bowling team. We bowled every Saturday morning. I wanted to quit bowling halfway through the season. I was out of cigarettes, and I used my bowling money to buy cigarettes for one week. Back then I could buy three packs of cigarettes for five dollars. I came back the following week, and I joined a new bowling team. My new team won the Championship that year. I was so happy that I won a first-place trophy for something in my life.

I wasn't popular at all with the girls during those years. I only had three girlfriends during those three years. Brenda, Mary, and Linda. Mary was the only one of the three that I wasn't too shy to approach. When I first saw her, I instantly wanted to spend some time with her. It wasn't a big deal since it's really nothing real at that age anyway.

During the summer between eighth grade and ninth grade I got myself into a lot of trouble. I was always in a lot of trouble at home, but that was because of my abusive stepdad, not because I was actually doing anything wrong, until now.

The kid I mentioned earlier about influencing me to like the Bengals was back in our neighborhood. Mike was a serious troublemaker. I wasn't at that time. I was just dealing with strict and abusive parents.

We were hanging out together quite a bit. Mike lived next door, and I could hang out with him since it didn't involve me leaving my yard too far. One night Mike said we should go out and do something. I said, yes. I had no idea what he had in mind though.

Mike walked around town that night, and he slashed people's car tires with a knife. I didn't know what to do or think. I didn't slash any tires, but I stayed with him all night while he slashed thirty-two car tires. That night was also the first time I ever witnessed a kid smoking weed. I didn't do it. I only smoked cigarettes. I may have been quiet and shy during that time, but deep inside of me, I had a bad attitude towards authority. I guess I didn't have much of a problem with what we were doing that night. If I remember right, I even thought it was kind of funny. It turned out to be not so funny. We read the newspaper the next day, and we saw all of the reports about the tires being slashed. We saved the newspaper.

It was a few days later, Mike and I were at another neighbor's house, and we were listening to the adults tell stories about dumb stuff that they did when they were younger. Mike looked at me, and he said, should we tell them?

I don't know what I was thinking, but I said, yeah.

We told the neighbors about slashing the car tires. Later on, that day, the neighbor women told my mom about what we said. When I got home, I immediately got beaten with a belt by my stepdad. Every time I got abused by my stepdad, he made me take off all my clothes. That way it hurt me and bruised me a lot more. After that, he took me to the police station, and turned me in to the police.

The officer told me to tell him what happened, and he would help me. I told him everything, but he didn't help me with anything. I was a juvenile delinquent.

On June 24th, 1989, I had to go to court for slashing car tires. I got put on probation, I received community service, I had a fine to pay, and I got thirty days in the youth center. I hated it in there because it was so boring, and time went so slow. I was away from my family though. I guess I liked that part about it.

After I got out of the youth center, I spent the rest of the summer doing my community service working at the cemetery to pay for the car tires that were damaged. I had two hundred hours of community service to do, and that wasn't very fun.

Mike was pissed off at me for getting him into trouble. It was his idea to brag about it to the neighbors, not mine. I guess he didn't want to take responsibility for himself. I thought it was funny, in 2011, after not seeing him since 1989, Mike contacted me on Facebook, and he was still bitching, and blaming me about him getting into trouble for that.

Thinking about it now, it would have been so easy to get away with that. All I had to say is, we read about the tire slashings in the newspaper, so we said that we did it so we could fit in with the neighbors when they were telling their stories. I am sure that I just told the truth because I knew how bad things were for me at home, and I didn't want to make things any worse for myself. Well, telling the truth was worse for me, so maybe that was one time I should have lied to save myself.

It wasn't even a year later, and I was in trouble again. I was turned into the police again by my stepdad. I was considered an unruly child. This time I was turned in because I stayed out too late, and I didn't have permission.

This time I got beaten with a belt by my stepdad, and I spent the weekend in the youth center. I didn't just get one or the other, I got both.

When my probation officer asked me where I was, I made up a crazy story about being attacked, and locked in the trunk of a car. I don't know why I said that, but I thought it sounded like a good excuse for me to not be able to get home on time. The mistake I made was mentioning a friend of mine in my story. When my probation officer checked my story, he found out that I was lying.

That was my opportunity to tell someone what was really going on at home, but I didn't take advantage of it. I should have told my probation officer that I was being abused at home, and maybe he could've helped me. I didn't say a word though. I guess it's a lot easier to think of the right things now that I should have done back then.

I don't know why I never said anything, but there are some people who needed to take responsibility for their bullshit and pay for it.

The truth is, I found a good hiding spot, and I was hiding that night. I noticed when I started Jr high school when I was walking home from school, there was a tunnel in the yard by the Jehovah Witness church. The tunnel went under the road, and it drained into the Sandusky River. I looked in the tunnel one day, and I instantly thought it would be a good hiding spot. It was dirty, wet, smelly, and gross in there, but I hid in there a lot of times when things were bad for me at home. I knew no one would ever find me in there. I couldn't tell anyone the truth about where I was that night I didn't get home on time. I couldn't tell anyone where my hiding spot was. I always felt safe there. That should tell you how bad it was for me at home if I felt safe in a drainpipe that was gross and had wild animals in there.

While I was in the youth center at that time, my dad came to visit me, but I told the guard that I didn't want to see anyone. I didn't know why my dad showed up to see me, he never tried to see me any other time. I don't know how anyone even knew that I was there.

My dad came back the next day during visiting hours, and again, I said that I didn't want to see anyone. The guard said, my dad needs to talk to me because he has a plan to help me. I didn't know what he meant by that, so I agreed to see him.

My dad said to me that there was a plan for me to leave home, and I was going to live with my uncle Ben. I don't know how that came about, but I thought that was a great idea because my uncle Ben was my favorite uncle. When I went to court on that Monday, it didn't happen though. I went back home with my abusive stepdad and my mom. I don't remember if I had the chance to say anything, but I should have told the judge what I was going through at home. That was my best chance to say something and get help. I didn't say a word though.

I believe it was that day in court that everyone in my family thought the worst about me, and that I was a bad person. I don't think that anyone really knew that I wasn't the problem, and I was just doing what I had to do to protect myself. I believe that day is when everyone in my family gave up on me.

My Jr high school years were a crazy time for me. I knew I had to make some changes before I got into high school. The first thing I did was cut my hair short and change my image. I started wearing shirts with my favorite sports teams on them. I even started wearing dressier clothes. I just knew I had to do something different.

I turned sixteen in August before I started high school. Within those three weeks, I got a work permit, and I got a job working at Burger King before school started. That is how I was affording new clothes. I was buying my own clothes. That was the first time in my life that I had nice clothes and shoes to wear. I definitely looked a lot better with short hair, and a new look. I needed to change with the times.

I was ready for high school. I was excited for something new. I felt like I was being fake with my new image, but maybe I was just finally finding myself. Maybe it was a good thing.

Things didn't quite go as planned though. I was happy with my new image, I was working hard at Burger King, but I didn't care much about school. I don't remember exactly what I was thinking, but it wasn't good.

I took Algebra in my sophomore year, and I was not good at it at all. I got a tutor to help. Kent was my tutor, but I really wasn't trying very much. I think Kent knew that, and he knew that I just wanted to copy his homework. Halfway through my sophomore year, I completely gave up on all of my classes. I didn't care. I was doing so bad in Algebra, my teacher made fun of me in front of the entire class multiple times. I guess he thought that was okay to do to a student. He even hit me once.

There was a rumor about my Algebra teacher, and one day someone put a piece of paper on his desk with a joke on it directed towards him referring to the rumor. He instantly thought that I did it, and he hit me with a book, and kicked me out of class. Jeff is the one who put the joke on his desk, I think. I should have said something about him teasing me and hitting me, but I was so used to not saying anything, I didn't that time either. I had a bad habit of letting people walk all over me and get away with stuff that they shouldn't.

I was doing as little as possible in school, and only focusing on working during my first year in high school. I was just going to school because I had too.

With my new image, I was doing better with the girls. I was excited about that. I dated two girls during my first year. Dawne and Leslie. That made me feel good about myself.

My second year went a lot better. I decided to try a lot harder. The first thing I did was take classes I knew I could do better in. The rest of my classes weren't too bad, but I needed to take an easier math class. I took a basic math class, but I still had the same asshole teacher from the year before. Well, I showed him that I could do a lot better when I was taking a class that I could handle.

My favorite class was third period English. I had a huge crush on my teacher. I did better in that class than I have ever done before in my life. I always liked it when we could write whatever we wanted. I turned in some very creative writing. I was into writing song lyrics during that time. I thought I wrote some very good stuff.

There was one day in the morning before school started, I was by my locker, and she came up behind me. She bumped up against me, and she said, "Why weren't you in class yesterday?

I told her that I went to a concert the night before so I couldn't make it to school. She smiled at me, and said, "I go to concerts, and I always come to school the following day. I had a bigger crush on her after that day. Thinking about it now, I should have told her that I liked her. She ended up married to a student.

I was doing okay with the girls though. I met Kathy Gassner while I was working at Burger

King. We dated for about six months when I was seventeen.

I felt like I was a fraud when I was dating Kathy. She was so intelligent. She was always talking about going to Ohio State after she graduated from high school. Me, I was barely getting through high school. We went to different schools, so she didn't know that. Kathy went to a Catholic school, and I didn't. I used chewing tobacco during that time, and she didn't know that. I don't think she would've liked it if she knew about it.

A week after we started dating, I was M.I.A. the following weekend. I am just glad that we didn't have any plans, and it didn't ruin anything. I definitely didn't want to mess that up. Kathy was great.

I was having trouble at home. My stepdad was bullying me about something. I can't remember what that was about. I just remember him coming after me. As soon as he stepped into my bedroom, I picked up my baseball bat, and I swung it at him. I had enough. I said, don't ever touch me again. I was finally fed up with his abuse, and I started standing up for myself. It was good that I started doing that, but he called the cops on me, and I was charged with being unruly again.

So, I spent the weekend in the youth center again. He never hit me again after that though. I was considered a mean and violent person by him since that incident. Apparently, it was only okay when he was beating on me. I called Kathy on Monday when I got out of the youth center, and everything was okay.

One day while I was working at Burger king, Kent stopped in, and he noticed Kim and he asked about her. Kim was my girlfriend Kathy's twin sister. So, Kent and I were dating twin sisters at one point during high school.

We may have gone in different directions, but Kent was the only friend that I had that was in and out, but still always around during all twelve of my school years. I am thankful for that. I always admired Kent. He had a nice family, and he had goals in life. After high school, he went on to become a police officer. Kent always knew what he was doing.

I saw Kent about a year ago for the first time in about thirty years, and I didn't even recognize him. He said hi to me, and he said his name because I didn't know who he was when he first approached me.

During the summer of my senior year, well actually I was a little behind, so I wasn't technically a senior, but I did turn eighteen, and I got my driver's license. I did it all from August 6th until the end of August when school started. I got my permit, I took my driver's test, and I bought a vehicle. All in a few weeks, and all on my own.

I couldn't do it any sooner. I was working a lot plus going to school so I couldn't take driver's education classes. So, I just waited, and did it when I was eighteen.

I bought my first vehicle on my own. I bought a Chevy truck from my friend, Randy. I paid for it from working at Burger King. I thought that I was doing very well doing everything on my own. That first truck I bought was the only Chevy I ever drove. I was always a Ford guy after that. I just got a good deal on that first truck from a friend. I just bought the first vehicle that I could afford.

I really had no idea what I was doing about the future after high school at that point, so I thought about going into the Army. I thought that was a great idea. That idea only lasted a few months because in December of 1992, I got the thought running through my head, I am eighteen, why am I still even going to school? I could've been doing a lot of other things. I know getting a better paying job was my first though.

I didn't stay out of school very long, and then I went back to school. I missed too many days, and I still didn't finish on time. I just knew that I had a very bad attitude at that time, and I really didn't know what I was doing.

I was lost again. I didn't know where I was heading. I wasn't off to a good start as an adult. I believe that was because of the way I was treated at home. I didn't have any confidence. I didn't feel good enough. I didn't think I was capable of doing good things in my life. My thinking was really messed up. I didn't know it until recently, but being abused like I was as a child, it can cause self-esteem issues. It can cause trauma. It can cause everything I was going through, but I just didn't realize it yet.

I ended up leaving Burger King, I started working at a factory job, called Sol Tech. It was a fiber glass factory. It was somewhere to start, I guess. I ended up living at home until I was twenty years old. Things weren't too bad since I was working a lot and taking care of myself during that time. My family's bullshit was far from over though.

WHAT THE HELL JUST HAPPENED

In August of 1997, after I split up with my wife, I was roommates with my brother Nick. I'm not sure why I did that. I could've stayed in my house by myself. My house was bigger, and a lot cheaper than my brother's place was. I don't know, I guess I didn't think I could do it on my own.

My brother and I always got along. We were both working so much at that time, we really didn't see much of each other.

Everything was going good with us living together, at least I thought so. There weren't any issues that I was aware of for the first two years.

On August 16th, 1999, I had some friends over to play cards and drink some beer. My friends Matt, Glenn, Sara, Celisa, and my brother were there. We were all having fun, but during the night my brother started acting drunk and stupid. We were at the kitchen table playing cards, my brother picked up a pair of scissors, and he was teasing Celisa by cutting at her hair with the scissors. After a couple of times, Celisa was getting aggravated by it. She turned to me, and she asked me to make him stop it. I didn't say anything wrong, I just said that she didn't want him to do it anymore.

After I said that, my brother turned to me, and he started bitching and yelling at me. By what he was saying, there was a problem that I didn't know about. Or he was just trying to look cool in front of everyone.

When my brother started yelling at me, I stood up. We were only a few feet apart to start with, but when I took a step closer, he pushed me backwards. I wasn't expecting that. I gained my balance, I walked towards him, I raised my arm, and I easily put him into a headlock.

I took my brother down to the floor in the kitchen immediately. When he tried fighting to get up, I just tightened the headlock up so he couldn't move.

It was kind of funny, he was always bragging about being a big badass Marine, but he couldn't even escape a simple headlock. It is true that if you can control someone's head like that, you can control their whole body, and there isn't anything they can do about it.

I was holding him in the headlock on the floor for about fifteen minutes. I was kind of getting bored holding him there, but I wasn't going to let up until he stopped raising hell.

Finally, my friend Glenn pulled me off of my brother. I had to let go then, Glenn was over three hundred pounds, and I couldn't hold on with that much weight pulling me. When I stood up, my brother got up quick, and he ran to his bedroom. When he came back out, he had a gun.

I wasn't a big fan of guns. I don't know anything about guns, and I didn't even know my brother had a gun. Nick was yelling, I am going to shoot you all.

Everyone ran outside, and my brother ran outside after everyone. When everyone, including me, saw him coming outside, we all ran down the street. My brother was standing in the yard shooting, and we were all running down the street trying not to get hit. Glenn was overweight and didn't run very fast so that was kind of amusing. We had to stop so he could catch up.

I didn't realize it at first, but Sara and Celisa weren't running with the rest of us. They were standing behind my brother. It didn't take long to figure out what the problem was.

I was actually dating Sara at that time, but when I wasn't around, she was turning my brother against me. I was dating her, but she was using my brother for money. I dated her a couple of times, and I knew how she was. I didn't know exactly what was going on during that time yet though.

While we were running down the street, a police car drove by, and she stopped when she saw us in the street. The officer asked, "What's going on? I pointed back, and I said, he has a gun, and he is shooting at us. The officer saw my brother because he was still in the yard shooting. The officer drove closer to the house, and my brother ran back inside. We watched for a few minutes, and it didn't take long before more police cars came and surrounded the house with my brother inside.

My mom lived just a few streets away, so we ran there. I went inside, woke her up, and I told her what was going on. My mom started yelling at me, but I didn't have any idea why. Sara and Celisa showed up at my mom's house about ten minutes later than the three of us did.

Obviously, I couldn't go back to the house because it was surrounded by cops, so I had to stay at Sara's mom's house with her that night. I didn't even have any shoes with me. I didn't have any time to put any on, so I ran down the street that night with no shoes on.

The next day I went back to the house to go on with my day as usual. Later on, that day I went over to my mom's house, and it was strange that Sara was there. I asked her, "What are you doing here? She had some dumb excuse, but that is when I knew for sure that she was the problem. I am sure that she was telling my mom and stepdad some bullshit story.

A few days after the incident happened, I received court papers. I had to appear in court because my family got a restraining order against me. They were saying that I was a mean and violent person. I just laughed about that.

I remember in court, I said, thanks your honor, you are actually doing me a favor. The judge asked what I meant by that. I replied, this guy sitting here has been abusing me for many years, and now this is the second time when he stood up for the criminal and betrayed the victim. I was a child when everything else happened, and I didn't know what to do. Now I was twenty-five, and I said what needed to be said. I didn't care about the restraining order, and I walked out of the courtroom.

There were a lot of backlashes from this. I had to figure out a new place to live. My trust issues got a lot worse after that. I became very bitter and angry. I wasn't quiet and shy anymore; I became very edgy. I was probably a little out of control after that. I didn't realize it for a while, but when my family turned their backs on me, it hurt me a lot. My depression started, but I didn't know it yet. It started a very dark time for me.

During the restraining order, I didn't get to see my kids for a while. My stepdad denied it later on, but I know it was his influence that I didn't get to see my kids so that way he felt like he had control over my kids.

The shooting incident really changed me, and not for the best. I was lost, and it got very dark for me. I had no idea what was to come, and I definitely wasn't ready for it.

WELCOME TO MY FAMILY

I still can't believe that the people who were supposed to love me and care about me the most, are the ones who hurt me, abandoned me, and betrayed me the most. That is a little wrong if you ask me.

There have been times when I was talking about things that bothered me to family members about things that other family members did or said to me, and I always get the impression that no one cares about anything I have to say. There have been times when I said something, and they stick up for the person who did me wrong. I am not like anyone else. I only tell the truth. I can't believe people seriously stand up for wrong over what's right. It makes me believe that I can't talk to anyone in my family about anything that bothers me. It appears that they won't listen or believe the truth anyway. Well, I am going to tell the truth whether anyone likes it or not.

I am currently eight months away from being fifty years old. My dad has never, and I mean never tried to reach out to me or get to know me. He knows the basics, my name, my birthday, everyone knows that I like the Steelers, and he may know another thing or two about me, but that's it.

My dad never contacted me on my birthday. He never contacted me on any Christmases. He never contacted me on any other day of the week during my whole life. It is not my fault that we never had a good relationship since it started when I was very young. There have been times when other family members said that I should call him. I am going to say right now, I am not going to do that. My dad had plenty of time to get to know me, but he chose not to.

My dad has said to me in the past that it was my mom's fault that I didn't hear from him when I was little. I can understand that because that happens. However, I have been an adult since 1992, and since then he couldn't blame my mom anymore, but he still never tried to reach out to me and get to know me. So, his excuses didn't make sense anymore. I stopped believing him since it didn't add up anymore.

I can seriously only remember a few conversations with my dad in my lifetime. One time was in 1996, and my girlfriend at that time and I went to see him to invite him to our wedding. It was going to be small, so we went to invite him in person. After we invited him, his response was, he would only go if my mom wasn't there. We both thought that was kind of shitty of him. It seemed like he was making it about himself. He didn't need to bring his issue with my mom into something that was about Heather and me. Over the years, my dad took every chance he could to take cheap shots towards my mom, but I never in my life heard her say anything about him. In 1996, their relationship had been over for like twenty years, but I guess he was dwelling on something that didn't matter anymore.

The next conversation I can recall was in the year 2000. My dad was talking about the bass guitar, and I mentioned the first bass guitarist that popped into my mind, Gene Simmons from Kiss. The only thing my dad had to say to my comment was, he called Gene Simmons a purple haired faggot. Nice huh? I don't like that word. Gene Simmons has never had purple hair, and he isn't gay. I didn't respond to that because I found it offensive.

The next conversation I remember was in 2014. There was a rare time when my dad, my brother, and I were all in the same room at the same time. My brother and I were talking, and I mentioned that Dwight Yoakam was going to be in concert in Toledo.

My dad chimed in and said, why would anyone want to go see him, he doesn't have any talent. I don't understand it. Maybe he likes to put down and talk trash about famous millionaire musicians.

I found it interesting that he says things like that. He makes comments like he thinks that he is better than everyone else. My dad seriously comes off like he is an arrogant person.

In 2020 on my birthday, my aunt Dorothy said happy birthday to me on Facebook. My dad commented on what she said, and he left a comment that said he has been trying to get ahold of me. That was not true. I never received a text message or a phone call from him. I guess he just left that comment to try and make himself look good because my aunt said happy birthday to me, and he didn't.

When I was younger, I thought my dad was cool. He has long hair, and he rides a Harley. I have always thought that style was cool. As years went on, I didn't think he was so cool anymore. I don't think anyone is cool if they never cared about me.

In 1994, I was driving to the gas station. I was very close to being out of gas, and I wasn't sure if I was going to make it without running out of gas. Well, I made it to the gas station, but I ran out of gas before I got to the gas pump. I had to push my car across the parking lot so I could get some gas. While I was pushing my car to the pump, I saw my dad at the gas station. He was getting gas. I saw him look directly at me while I was pushing my car. My dad didn't say anything to me. He didn't offer any help. He just watched me push my car across the lot to the pump. I filled up my car with gas, and I went on with the rest of my day. I always thought that was shitty of him to just watch me struggle like that.

There were a couple of times when I was in a jam, and I lived with my dad for a while. I never asked him for anything in my life. It was his wife's idea when I stayed with them two times. Neither time ended very well. There have been times when I was around my dad for long periods of time, but he never talked to me or had anything to say to me. I found that strange.

The first time I lived with my dad was in 2000-2001. I wasn't doing very well at that time so somehow; I ended up staying there for a while.

When I was doing better, I told them I was moving out. I have no idea why, but my dad's wife started screaming at me. I couldn't figure that out. I wasn't obliged to stay there any longer. While she was yelling, I said one thing about eating, I believe, and she said, oh I guess I'm a bitch. So, my dad was getting mad at me for something that I didn't even say. His wife was just saying stupid shit. It was uncalled for drama if you ask me.

The next time I lived with them for a while was when I returned home from Tennessee. I didn't want to stay with them because I remembered what happened the other time I stayed with them, and I didn't want something like that to happen again. Again, I didn't ask them for anything, but my dad's wife demanded that I stay with them. So, I did.

I was doing my share, I was paying to stay there, but one week there was a mistake at work, and my paycheck was a couple hundred dollars short. Just for one week I didn't have much money, but I could've made it up the following week. My dad's wife was screaming at me over that, and seriously putting me down for something that wasn't my fault. That made absolutely no sense to be acting that way.

I packed up my stuff, and I left there with nowhere to go. I wasn't going to put up with craziness like that. I didn't need it. I guess my dad stands up for wrong over right because I am sure that he never stuck up for me.

After I left there, I received several letters left on my car while I was at work. They were left by my dad's wife. The letters were nonsense.

She was putting me down, threatening me, and she admitted that she was going to try and take my daughter from me. All of that bullshit because there was one mistake with my paycheck at work.

The next time I saw my dad was about a year later. I went up to him to say something to him, and his wife was trying to act nice since my dad was there. I told him about the letters, and about her threatening me, but she denied it, and she lied to my dad. I just said, whatever, and I walked away. I didn't know it before then, but now I knew that my dad didn't know anything about the letters.

My dad had almost fifty years to get to know me if he wanted to, but I guess he doesn't want to, or he would have done it many years ago. When I was younger, it really didn't bother me at all. I never gave it any thought whatsoever.

Around 2017, I think it started to bother me. I messaged my dad one night when I was drunk, things were bothering me, and I asked him, why don't you ever reach out to me and talk to me.

After I messaged him, he contacted me one time, and that's it. I guess he thought one time was good enough even though I messaged him, and I asked him why he never has.

Now, it doesn't bother me at all. I don't care about someone who has never tried to get to know me. I am never going to mention him again after I finish this story. I am done, and I am over it. It is his loss, not mine. I seriously don't care about him at all anymore. I hope my dad is proud of himself that he has a child that hates him now.

Now, on to some more family craziness. After the shooting incident, my brother was in the county jail for a year. My brother was charged with firing a gun in the city limits, or something like that. After he was released from jail, I was in court again because my stepdad cancelled the restraining order. After court that day, my mom and stepdad tried to talk to me, but I just kept walking away from them. I didn't have anything to say to them. It was strange though, there was never a problem between my brother and me after that incident. No one in my family ever brought up the shooting incident again. I guess they just wanted to act like it didn't happen. I guess acting like something didn't happen is what people do when they know they were wrong.

My brother did his time, and the whole thing was over. I always wondered why my brother didn't tell the truth now and say that none of that was my fault. He could have proved that all the hell I was going through was really unnecessary.

It was in September of 2001, and I wasn't doing very well at that time when the restraining order was lifted. It was because my family betrayed me why I wasn't doing very well.

About a month after the restraining order stopped, I was talking to my family again. I think the reason is because I wanted to see my little brother, Mark. We were very close before that happened, and I missed him.

In 2002, my family moved to Tennessee, and then I didn't have to worry about them anymore. Then, in September of 2003, I made the dumbest mistake of my life, I followed them to Tennessee.

I wasn't doing very well in Tiffin, so I wanted a change of scenery, I guess. My mistake was that I followed the people that played a big part in why I wasn't doing well at that time. My mental health was off the charts at that point, but I moved down there anyway. I guess I thought things would be okay, but they definitely were not.

I wasn't even down there for a month, and things went bad. My family moved down there because my stepdad was going to start a construction business. I should have known better, but I went down there to work for him, and that didn't work out too well.

We were working on a job, and he started bullying me. It was always like that doing anything with him. He doesn't explain anything, but he bitches when something isn't done his way. Less than a month down there, he was bullying me on a job, and I wasn't going to put up with him after the third time that day. I said, don't talk to me like that, and I started walking. I had no idea where I was, or where I was going, but I wasn't going to stay around my stepdad, and his bullshit.

It took me a while, but eventually I got back home, but it was the next day. It took me the rest of that day, and all night, but I made it home.

He always acted like doing something his way was the only way, but that isn't the case in any situation.

The next time on the job, I was doing something just fine my way, but I guess he felt the need to bully me, and he started screaming at me at a customer's house. He was seriously acting crazy. I just dropped what I was doing, and I said, fuck you, and I walked home again. At least this time it was a lot closer to home than the last time. I was never going to put up with his bullshit ever again, and I didn't. He would never take responsibility for his actions either. The best way to describe my stepdad is, he acts just like Charles Manson. He seriously felt like he had to have control over everyone. He didn't like it very much if he wasn't in control of someone in the family. Yes, it was usually me who wouldn't let him control me.

I was suspended a few different times while I was working for him. It was never for too long because he needed me. I wouldn't let him treat me like shit. My brother-in-law Tim let him get away with his crap. He let my stepdad run him down a lot. One day my stepdad even threw a circular saw at Tim.

I didn't learn anything from my stepdad the whole time I was working for him. I learned everything from Tim. It was a lot easier learning from someone who wasn't an asshole about everything, and who talked and explained everything instead of bitching all the time.

My stepdad's work always looked bad. He rushed through everything, and he didn't care. He only cared about money. He got sued because of his work twice, and he didn't even take responsibility for it. He blamed me one time over a little speck of paint.

The truth is, there were a lot of times when he wouldn't even show up at some jobs. He sat on his ass while Tim and I did all the work. A customer wanted something a certain way, but he wasn't around so a women got tired of it, and she found anything wrong to sue him. I know the details because I was there every day doing my job. I am surprised that he didn't get sued more than two times. His work wasn't very good.

Most days while Tim and I were busy working, my stepdad just told his bullshit exaggerated stories to the homeowners. He was the biggest liar I have ever met in my life. One time he tried to include me in the story he was telling, but I didn't play along with his lie, and I made him look really stupid. I thought it was funny.

By 2010 the construction business was about out of business. I moved on to do other things. If there was a small job to do, I didn't do it because my stepdad started ripping us off.

Then, all hell broke loose. My stepdad was telling my mom that he was going out of town to work for a different company. There were times when he was gone for days, or a week at a time. One day my sister called me, and she told me where he was really going when he was gone, and it wasn't to work. My sister told me that her dad has been going to see a former girlfriend of my brother's, and they have been spending a lot of time together. I have no idea why she told me about that. I don't agree with the stupid shit that they all do. I did the right thing. I went and I told my mom. After I told my mom, she didn't believe me, and she started screaming at me. She was wondering why I would say something like that.

That is the way it always went though. She always stood up for her piece of shit husband, and she wouldn't listen to the truth. I was somehow the bad guy for telling her what I knew. It was crazy how I was always the bad guy to my family when someone else messed up.

I feel like I'm in one of those movies where everyone thinks that the main character is crazy because of the story they are telling. In the end of the movie, we always find out the one everyone else thinks is crazy, is the only one telling the truth.

My grandma May was living down in Tennessee also during that time. She had a safe with all of her valuables in it. One day her safe was broken into, and when the police officer was asking questions about the incident, my stepdad was accusing a friend of my younger brother. When the officer asked my grandma how much cash was in the safe, before she had the chance to answer, my stepdad made his mistake, and he answered with the right amount of money. I guess no one else picked up on that, but my grandma did. She knew immediately who stole her money. My stepdad did it. It was an inside job.

When we were working construction, we did a lot of work for a nice older women named, Mrs. Brackett. I saw her one day at the grocery store a couple of years after the construction business was over. She came over to me, and she said, sorry to hear about your niece. I wasn't sure what she was talking about. Then Mrs. Brackett said, my stepdad told her about my niece Nicole passing away in a car accident. I replied, no she didn't. We were both confused. Mrs. Brackett told me that my stepdad borrowed a lot of money from her so that he could go out of state to attend his granddaughter's funeral. He lied to a nice woman so he could scam her out of money. That is sick if you ask me.

That wasn't the end of his crime spree. He paid for what he did next. He started robbing places. He finally got caught after he robbed a bank. Seriously though, who in the hell would rob a bank while driving a work truck with his name and phone number on the side of it? After I heard that, I laughed so hard. I seriously thought it was funny. He was finally paying for something he did. I was glad that I didn't have to deal with him for a while.

My stepdad was a career criminal. He was a conman for as long as I have known him. That guy was obsessed with money, and would do anything to get it, except work hard for it.

From everything I have seen over the years, he was only successful from 2002-2010, other than those years he was a low life loser. He shouldn't have even had good years for those eight years. He was collecting disability for as long as I can remember, so he shouldn't have been running a construction business anyway. He did everything under the table so he wouldn't get caught. He never paid taxes. He was doing a lot of stuff illegally.

He was only in prison for five years, I believe. I hadn't seen him for the longest time. I had nothing good to say to him. He did contact me in 2019 after my grandma passed away. He only contacted me so he could bitch and talk trash.

He was blaming me because he and my sister didn't know about my grandma being in the hospital. That made no sense because I know he didn't really care about my grandma. He just cared about what he could steal from her house since she was gone. Once again, I was the bad guy for something stupid. I had nothing to say to him or my sister. I don't like either one of them, so I didn't want to tell them anything about my grandma.

Both of them have stolen a lot from my grandma over the years. They didn't need anything else. I already knew what I would get if something happened to her. I talked to my grandma a lot. I was the only one in the family who ever went to visit her. I went over to her house, and I cleaned for her every week to help her out.

The only reason anyone else went to see my grandma is when they wanted money from her. My sister always made up an excuse and saying the money was for an emergency, but my grandma wasn't dumb, everyone knows that my sister is on drugs.

My half-sister is exactly like her dad. She is okay with her lying bullshit, but she doesn't like the truth in return. I have always confronted her when she involved me in her bullshit. She always turned it around on me just like her dad always did. Kristi has always been a low life person on drugs. She always depended on government assistance. The one thing that pisses me off the most is, I was very good friends with Amy Ritchie for many years. I wasn't a fan of her drug use, but that was her choice. I know for a fact that my sister Kristi was supplying pills to Amy that lead to her death. I believe that she killed my dear friend. That still gets to me. I still miss Amy.

I never had anyone in my life to teach me anything. I never had anyone in my life I could turn to for advice about anything. There was a lot I just learned on my own. I was a horrible driver when I first started because I didn't know how to drive. Eventually I just got better at it.

I have nothing to say to anyone in my family who has ever done me wrong. I am over it all now, and I am never going to deal with any of them again. I don't want anything to do with anyone who abused me, abandoned me, or acted like they never cared about me. I am too old for any drama or bullshit now. I have moved on with my life, and I am at peace with everything now. I depend on myself. I have been shown that the people I should have been able to depend on, didn't care. Now, I don't care about anyone in my family who let me down. I promise I am not going to allow any family members to bring me down by their actions ever again. That is all I am going to say about that. It is too late now, and I seriously don't believe I want things to be right in any of the situations. I am sure there is a lot more I could have mentioned, but it's time to move on now.

I AM NOT OKAY

Everything I have said so far, and a lot of what I still have to say, all go together. Everything is heading in the same direction and leading to one thing. Feeling unwanted and not cared about by my dad, being abused as a child, mentally abused as an adult by my stepdad, and other things that happened to me were leading towards depression.

I wasn't very happy as a child, but I don't know for sure if I was depressed yet, so I believe my depression started on December 21st, 1996. That should have been the best day of my life. Actually, it was, but it was also the worst day of my life up until that point. The bad just overtook the good way too much.

My son Curtis was born on that day, but I also said goodbye to my hero, my grandpa, at his funeral earlier that same day. I was not okay after that day. Sometimes I just shut down from people around me, and sometimes I wasn't quiet and shy anymore. I was a lot more outspoken. It definitely wasn't a good way to be. I have never lost anyone before that I was that close to. I didn't take it very well. So, I didn't deal with it very well. The main thing I did wrong after my grandpa passed away was change so much that I pushed my wife at that time away.

Less than three years after my grandpa passed away, the shooting incident happened. I changed a lot more after what my family did to me because of that. When that happened, I became very bitter and angry. I was mad at the world. I even got a tattoo across my chest that says, me against the world. I could not focus or concentrate on anything during that time. I was just so pissed off because I was the victim in that situation, but I was being treated like I was a criminal. I was not handling that well at all. There were times when I thought about getting revenge somehow on my family for betraying me, but I didn't. That was probably a good thing. I just knew that I wasn't okay. I just knew that I had enough of them treating me bad all of my life.

In the year 2000, I was watching the movie Armageddon for the first time, and there was a scene in that movie that really got to me. It even made me a little teary eyed, and that wasn't normal for me. It was that exact moment when I knew that something more serious was wrong with me.

Finally, I decided to go to Fireland's, the mental health treatment center. I couldn't keep feeling the way that I had been feeling.

The first time I went there, I walked in, I talked to someone, and I told them everything. When I told them how angry I was, and I thought about getting revenge on my family, or possibly hurting myself, I guess that was a big red flag to them. They asked me if I felt like I needed to be hospitalized to get myself some help. All I knew was that I wasn't okay, and someone may get hurt. So, I agreed to go to the hospital. They transported me to the hospital to get things figured out for me.

It was something that I wasn't used to, so soon after I got there, I was screaming, get me the fuck out of here. I just remember someone saying, you have to stay so we can help you. I didn't care though. I just wanted to leave as soon as I got there. I felt like a prisoner or something. I wasn't the criminal. I didn't do anything wrong. I remember feeling like Michael Myers from the Halloween movies when he was in the mental hospital before he escaped. Being in there made me feel like I was crazy or something.

I didn't get to leave right away. I had to stay overnight. I guess I raised enough hell, so they let me leave the next day. I just didn't like that feeling of being in there. I didn't get anything out of that first hospital stay.

I wasn't a very pleasant person to be around at that time. I was with my daughter's mom during that time, and we weren't getting along at all. I wasn't an easy person to get along with during that time, but neither was she. The difference was, I was bitter, and I didn't trust anyone because of the things that happened to me. Her, she was just a lot of unnecessary drama. I found out she was going behind my back and staying in contact with my family and betraying me as well. That caused a lot of problems between us. She proved that she couldn't be trusted.

She had a violent side to her. I wasn't expecting it once when she hit me with something, and it cut my head open. After she did that, she called the police on me, but she was the one who was charged with domestic violence after the officer saw my head cut, and bleeding.

Not long after that, I was charged with domestic violence. I believe she was getting revenge on me because of her domestic violence charge, so she set me up.

We were arguing one day, but I really didn't want to be. Actually, I never wanted to be, but I never backed down. I didn't want to argue so I walked away. I had a can of Mountain Dew in my hand as I was walking away, and she said something stupid to me. I got pissed off, and I threw the can of Mountain Dew as I was walking away from her. There is no way in hell I can throw something without looking as I am walking away from like twenty feet away and hit her right in the face.

I was taken to jail after that. I knew I was set up because when I appeared in court the next morning, she was there with bandages on her face and hand. There is no way it did that much damage. There is no way both her face and hand could've been hurt. If she did get hit, it would have been one or the other, but not both.

I was getting used to it though. It was nothing new to me having someone betraying me. So, I knew I had to be more serious, and go back to Fireland's and get help for myself. I was ordered by the court to attend domestic violence classes at Fireland's, but I needed to work on my mental health as well. I had to try and take care of myself better.

Less than six months after the first time, I was back in the hospital. I stayed for the second time. I was there for five days during my second time. I attended the groups, and I participated. I was very quiet, but I listened to everything. I started on medication that was supposed to help me feel better.

I was like a ticking time bomb ready to go off at any time, and I didn't think anything was going to help me during that time. My thoughts were very wrong way too often. Not long after my second time, I was hospitalized for a third time. I believe it was for four days at that time.

I remember someone asked me why I needed to be hospitalized two times back-to-back like that. They said that I didn't need to be in the hospital that much like it was a bad thing that I was. I was in a very bad state of mind, and I guess people just don't understand mental health. I just knew that I was trying to figure out what was wrong with me. I didn't like feeling the way I was during that time in 2000-2001.

I wasn't really committed to going so I didn't continue going to Fireland's for services when I wasn't ordered to. I was not interested in doing anything that I didn't really have to do. Going into the hospital didn't help me at all. So, I just went on feeling the way I was.

I lived in Tennessee from 2003 to 2014. When I lived down there, I didn't reach out for any help with my mental health. I definitely needed it though. I didn't know a lot down there, and I wasn't even sure where to go for any help. I went through a lot of hell down there.

I was a mess when I returned back to Ohio in 2014. When I decided to come back, I didn't even have a plan in place. I just packed up what I could fit in my car, and I came back. I also had custody of my daughter, so I had to be careful with my decisions. My decision making wasn't always right when my mind wasn't right.

I was really lost. I couldn't stay in the situation that I was in, but I should've had a better plan. I came back, and I didn't even know where I was going to live. So, when I got to Ohio, I stayed in a few different places temporarily for a while. Nothing was working out for me, so I ended up staying at a homeless shelter for a short time. It wasn't too bad. It was a huge house with a lot of rooms, but there were a lot of other people there also. I just knew I had to be somewhere safe because I had my daughter.

We only stayed there for a week, and I found us a house to live in. I didn't have any money, no furniture, no food, but I had a house to live in. It didn't go very well. I had some things to figure out, but I couldn't turn the house down.

My thoughts were very bad, and I knew I wasn't taking care of my daughter very good anymore. I always did a great job with her before, but it was completely different this time. I started working at a new job after we moved into the house, but it didn't last long. I was betrayed by someone else I thought was a good friend.

In 2015, my life was flipped upside down once again. The house I moved into was right beside the women that was in charge of the homeless shelter. I don't believe that was just a coincidence that it was right beside her house. She was still helping us after we moved into the house, and out of the homeless shelter. I didn't know it at first, but I think she had a plan for what she was doing. She wanted to feel like she was in control of me or something.

The reason I think that is, she hooked up with guys from the homeless shelter before, and she helped them, and betrayed them before. I saw that for myself. When I first moved in beside her, she had a guy that she met at the homeless shelter living with her, and she betrayed him.

I found a job, and I thought that we were going to be okay. I was at work one day, and Jenny texted me and she was bitching at me. She was all worked up, and she said there was a warrant out for me. I don't know how she knew that because I didn't even know it. I didn't know what was going on. I left work to go find out what was going on, but my mental health was so bad at that time, I checked myself into the hospital. I just knew that I wasn't thinking right, and I needed to get my mind right.

I knew my daughter would be okay because we did have food during that time at home, and I thought Jenny would help me with her.

I was in the hospital for five days. I called Jenny for a ride home when it was time for me to leave. She came to pick me up, but when we arrived back in Tiffin, two police cars showed up to arrest me. I still didn't know what was going on, but she turned me in.

She said that I went into the hospital because I was trying to avoid being arrested, but that wasn't the case. I didn't know anything about the warrant other than what she said. I had no idea what was going on in the first place. I just knew that I wasn't okay.

I went to jail that day, but I was only there overnight. In court the next day, I finally figured out what was going on. There was a warrant out for me because I missed a therapy appointment at Fireland's, and that was part of my probation.

Jenny didn't even know why there was a warrant, she just knew there was one for me. So, she was freaking out over me just missing an appointment.

It didn't take long before everything got a lot worse for me. I was out of a job, I didn't have any food at home, I didn't have any money, and my daughter didn't even believe in me anymore.

Every other time, I figured things out, but this time I couldn't do it. It definitely didn't help since my daughter was influenced by someone else. I knew I wasn't doing what was best for her during that time. I knew I couldn't take care of her right when I wasn't okay myself and taking care of myself.

Jenny sort of took over my daughter, and there really wasn't anything I could do about it. I wasn't okay, and it was probably best that someone else was taking care of her.

That destroyed me, and I got a lot worse. I was in the hospital to get myself better another nine times in 2015. I lost everything, and I had no choice but to try harder now. It wasn't easy. I really didn't know where to start since my mental health was so bad. I couldn't even think straight, and it was very difficult to live a normal life. My daughter lost all faith in me, I guess. She wouldn't talk to me at all anymore. That made me keep sinking lower and lower.

Usually, I was in the hospital for five or seven days, but the last time I was in the hospital in 2015, it was for thirty-two days. I was very bad, and I wanted to give up and die by that point since I didn't have my daughter anymore.

I didn't explain everything to my daughter about what I was going through at that time because I didn't want her to worry about anything. Maybe I should have, so maybe she would've understood better. Maybe that would have helped, and things didn't need to be as bad between us.

Every time I went into the hospital, it felt like they just gave me new medication until I felt okay, and then they sent me home. I wouldn't allow that during my thirty-two-day stay. I needed to be better.

During that stay in the hospital, the doctor switched my medication every couple of days, but I didn't feel any better. That didn't make any sense to me because it takes longer than that to get into your system and work correctly. So, of course there isn't going to be any change within a day or two.

The doctor changed my medication one time, and I started seeing things that weren't really there. I swear I saw a ball of yarn one night, and it kept getting bigger and bigger. It filled up my whole room. I ran out of my room and ran to the nurse's desk. I was yelling, there is something in my room. The nurse went into my room, and she looked around, but she didn't see anything. I was freaking out, and I felt like I was seriously going crazy. It definitely wasn't normal.

Another time when my medication was changed, I felt something crawling all over me afterwards, and it wouldn't stop. I kept looking, but there wasn't anything on me. I kept feeling for it, but I didn't feel anything on me. That wasn't a pleasant feeling. It lasted for a couple of weeks even after I left the hospital. I felt like I was getting worse being in there, not any better.

The only thing that made me feel okay while I was there was talking to the therapist every day named Laura. I think that just made me feel okay because I liked talking to her because she was so damn sexy, and beautiful. I looked forward to seeing her every day.

For the last few days, the doctor sent me to another hospital to have shock therapy done on me. I was supposed to have that done twelve times I believe, but after I had it done one time, I didn't want to do that anymore. I didn't know what was happening to me while I was out during it. I didn't like that feeling of not knowing.

It was Thanksgiving when I told them that I didn't want to do it anymore. The nurse told me that I could leave if I called someone to come get me. So, I called my aunt Dorothy, and she came to get me. She didn't have a lot of time, but she did it. We went straight to Thanksgiving dinner after she picked me up. I didn't feel very comfortable being around so many people that soon. I didn't stay long, and I knew I had to leave. I went back to my empty house by myself.

The reason for my thirty-two-day hospital stay was because I was ready to give up on my life and die. I took a lot of my medication at once, and I was going to die that night.

When I started feeling bad and weak from taking all of the pills, I called 911 for some help. I guess I changed my mind about dying. The thought running through my head was, I would never have my daughter back in my life if I died. So, I chose to get help instead of dying.

I continued living in my empty house for a while. I didn't have any food. The bills were not being paid for a while. I was just existing, but I wasn't living a good life. I felt like I had no life left in me during that time. It was a very difficult time for me.

I tried working a couple of different jobs, but they didn't work out for me. My mind wasn't right, and I had very bad anxiety. I felt trapped or something every time I was anywhere during that time.

Finally, my case manager at that time at Fireland's got me into a group home. In there at least I felt safe, and I had three meals a day to eat. Having a curfew didn't bother me much since I wasn't going out in public much during that time anyway. I didn't want anyone to see me. I was ashamed of myself for sinking so low and allowing everything to get so bad.

My thoughts while I was living in the group home were, now I had time to figure things out, and I didn't need to worry so much. Worrying was what I did the most though. I had to get back on track somehow. I always figured things out before, and I thought I could do it again. I lived in the group home for about six months.

I saw a friend I hadn't seen in many years, and she mentioned that she had a spare room at her house, so I moved in with her. I felt like everything was going to be okay. I was living with a good friend, and Lynelle is someone I knew that I could trust.

I didn't know it ahead of time, but that house had a bad reputation. There was an overdose in that house, and someone died from it. There was a lot of traffic going in and out of that building. A lot of people around there were on drugs.

I am not a big fan of drugs, or anyone who does them. It was okay living there because I was around a friend that I could trust, but I stayed to myself when other people were around. I didn't trust anyone who came around there. While I was living there between 2017 and 2019, I had things stolen, and her daughters stole money from me. I thought I was being kind and helping them out, but I didn't know that my money was going towards drugs at first. I wouldn't have helped anyone if I knew that.

I wasn't court ordered to go to Fireland's at this point anymore. I was past that, but I was still going on my own. I have definitely been trying since 2017. I saw a therapist. I saw the doctor. I saw a case manager. I was even attending groups. There were times during 2016 to 2020 that I was going to Fireland's four or five days a week. Sometimes I didn't want to go, but I was determined to get myself better.

The next time I was hospitalized was at the end of 2018. I was being betrayed again by someone, and I wasn't doing very well. I was having serious anxiety attacks at that time.

I thought maybe going into the hospital could help me because it had been a couple of years, and maybe I needed a medication change or something. I was in there for five days at that time.

I stayed there at Lynelle's until July of 2019. I left there, and I stayed at the homeless shelter again for a few months. I didn't get down and out that time. Instead, I was getting prepared. The whole time I was staying there, I was trying to come up with a good plan. In November of 2019, I found my own place, and I was finally getting settled by myself. That is what I needed to do.

It was a different woman in charge of the homeless shelter at this time, and she told me about a place that I moved into after Thanksgiving in 2019.

I felt so much better about everything after I moved in by myself. I felt like I was safe. That was the main thing that I needed; I believe.

There was only one thing that I was doing during that time that wasn't right. I was doing okay going to my appointments at Fireland's, but there was one thing that I wasn't being honest about. I was still drinking a lot of alcohol, but I always told them that I wasn't.

When I was going to therapy, a lot of times I didn't feel like saying anything. Then, there were days when I had a lot to say if I was bitter about some dumb drama going on in my life. A lot of times I would talk to my therapist about movies that we liked, or that we have seen lately. It was interesting sometimes, and I liked talking about movies because I love watching movies, but a lot of times going to therapy wasn't doing much for me, I don't believe. I still went to every appointment though. I kept believing something good was going to happen. The reason I didn't believe it was helping me by going to therapy is, one day I asked him for advice dealing with something, and he said, that's not how therapy works. He doesn't have any advice for me.

I even asked him, so, what's the point of coming then? What do you do to help me? I was very confused. I guess he just listens to me, and that's all.

He was younger than me, and he was very intelligent. In the end, he did help me out a lot. He had some information that ended up changing my life forever. That story comes a little later.

I honestly believe that I was still holding onto things that happened to me years prior, and I was letting a lot of things that probably didn't matter anymore hold me back. I guess I didn't know how to move on anymore and move forward. Nothing should be holding me back, but I guess I was allowing it to happen. I was really lost in this world.

Maybe death isn't the greatest loss in life. Maybe it is what dies inside of us when we are still alive.

Currently, I do have a good mental health team at Fireland's, and they really help me. I have a therapist who is very intelligent, and he helps me out a lot, even when I don't have to see him on a regular basis. He really believes in me. I have a case manager who goes above and beyond for me. We joke around a lot, but she does a lot for me. I have the best nurse. I always like talking to her because she is so easy to talk to. She is very beautiful and sexy also. I think that is why I like seeing her. I have a great doctor. She is so easy to talk to, and she always makes me feel better about everything when I talk to her about serious issues. I couldn't ask for a better support team. I am so thankful that I have them all.

THAT THING CALLED LOVE

In 1995, I was doing okay. I was just working a lot and living my life. I was content. I was working at Sol Tech at that time, and in October of 1995, I met Heather. I switched from second shift to first shift, and I noticed Heather instantly. I had my eye on her, and I mentioned her to someone else one day. I didn't tell the guy to say anything to her, but I guess he just wanted to get involved in it for some reason. She said, something like, if I play my cards right. I don't know what that meant, and she said later, she doesn't know why she said that. It was kind of funny.

We decided to go out. After we did one time, we wanted to keep going out. We agreed to spend a lot of time together except for two days in October. I had a Monday night football game I was going to, and she had a Tracy Lawrence concert coming up that she was going to.

Everything was instantly going well. By February of 1996, we decided to live together.

Everything was great, and we got along well together. It wasn't long before we realized that we had a baby on the way. We were both so happy.

We wanted to get married before the baby arrived in December, so we got married on November 19th, 1996. It was small, but it was a great day for us.

Just a month into our marriage, we attended my grandpa's funeral on December 21st, 1996. That tore me up very badly. On our way home from the funeral, I had to pull over so I could break down. I did not take saying goodbye to my grandpa very well. We made it home, but I couldn't grieve for very long. We were in the hospital that same day because our son was about to be born. That was the coolest thing to me. I said goodbye to my grandpa, and he was replaced on the same day with my son. That was the happiest day for us.

We were stressed around that time, I remember. We definitely had a lot going on at once, and it was about Christmas time. I wasn't the same anymore though. I was devastated about losing my grandpa. I guess the birth of my son couldn't overcome that enough for me.

We were perfect together up until that point. After losing my grandpa, there were times when I just wanted to be left alone, and there were times when we weren't getting along anymore. Everything changed on that day. I didn't even realize it, but I wasn't the same anymore.

We kept going for a while longer, but we weren't doing so well. We separated on August 25th, 1997. We were still talking, and getting along after we separated, but it was too late to fix it. Yes, I changed that much. I take full responsibility for how much I changed.

The real problems started years later, but she doesn't take responsibility for anything she has done wrong. It doesn't make sense to me, but okay if that's the way she really is. I found out later on that she isn't the person I once knew.

I ended up moving to Tennessee, but I saw my son every chance I could even though he was two states away. There were times when I was talking to Curtis, and he told me about his mom's new husband hitting him. I was not happy about that, so I asked her about that. There were times when Curtis was in trouble, and he spent time in the youth center. I didn't know what was going on, but there was something going on that she wasn't saying. As far as I knew, my son could have been going through something similar to what I went through as a child.

After I was living down in Tennessee for a couple of years, Heather called me, and she asked me if I wanted Curtis for good. I instantly said, hell yes. She said that she was going to do it legally so I would have him.

After a while, I called Heather, and I asked her when I was going to receive legal papers for having Curtis. She said she was working on it.

After a while I started not to trust her because I never received the papers, and I eventually took Curtis back to her. I didn't want to, but something didn't seem right to me. I didn't know what to think.

It was very difficult dealing with my son. He had bad anger issues as a child, and fighting with him every day wasn't very fun. Even after I took Curtis back to his mom, she was still calling me, and wanting me to take him. Heather even said that she didn't want him in her house anymore because he was destroying her family. I always thought that comment was kind of crazy, because she said it like Curtis wasn't a part of her family anymore.

I got Curtis back when it was legal. It was done on her terms though. She wouldn't even pay any child support for Curtis.

When I had my son, I did find out what the real problem was. It was Curtis himself. Sometimes I had no choice but to fight back to protect myself. I had no idea ahead of time because she never told me anything. So, when I had him, I was dealing with the same thing that she was dealing with, and it wasn't pleasant.

I was having a lot of problems with my son when I had him, and eventually it got very bad. We had a court hearing in 2013 to figure out what was best for Curtis. Heather went down to Tennessee to attend the hearing, and instead of telling the truth, and doing what was right, she just said anything to make herself look good.

She did everything possible to make me look bad.

The truth is, Heather went through the same exact thing as I did dealing with our son, and she handled him by basically kicking him out of her house and sending him to me so she wouldn't have to deal with him anymore. She wouldn't tell the truth about herself, or at least back me up because she knew how difficult he was.

Also, if I wasn't doing good with Curtis when I had him, she had the chance to get him back that day in court, but again she said that she didn't want him back. If she said that she didn't want him back in a courtroom, how does that make her any better than me? It doesn't make her any better, but she doesn't tell anyone about what she said or done wrong.

I admit that I probably didn't handle everything with my son the right way, but neither did his mom. The difference is, I'm not afraid to admit it.

The reason I know she tells a bullshit side of the story is, when I returned to Ohio in 2014, I heard the rumors about what she was saying about me.

I have been harassed, threatened, and assaulted by people because of her bullshit. I ran into an old friend of mine who is now a friend of my ex-wife, and I guess she doesn't like me anymore because of the lies and drama. Heather always leaves out the part about what she did wrong though. That is the way it goes in today's society. People put other people down, but they keep the truth about themselves a secret.

I don't ever say anything about my first ex-wife because I don't care what she does. I haven't cared since we divorced in January of 1998. I guess she feels the need to keep drama going by saying dumb shit about stuff that hasn't mattered for a long time now. I guess she loves drama that much. I got tired of the bullshit and being harassed because of her lying drama for the past ten years, so I confronted her about it recently. She still won't admit her bullshit. That is kind of sad that she is okay with her bullshit, but not the truth. I don't need to put anyone else down in order to make myself look good or feel better like she does. It never made any sense to me because my son's issues were about him, not Heather or I, but she makes everything about herself.

I loved it down in Tennessee. The bullshit I went through wasn't great, but everything else was nice. I lived between Knoxville and Gatlinburg, and that area had so much to do. It was a huge tourist area. I went to Gatlinburg and Pigeon Forge as often as I could. We did a lot of work in that area also. There was always a lot of construction going on in that area. Something new was always being built.

I was only down in Tennessee exactly one week, and while we were doing a job in the mountains, I saw a bear close by, and later that same day, there was a black panther walking down the street. That was very cool.

Soon after I moved down to Tennessee, I realized that I was allergic to seafood. My favorite food used to be shrimp, but not since 2003. I was eating at a seafood restaurant one evening, and I was eating shrimp. Later that night I started feeling very sick, and my face swelled up. I was rushed to the hospital, but I didn't know what was wrong. After I told the doctor that I ate shrimp, he said that I had an allergic reaction to it. That was difficult to hear, and I couldn't eat my favorite food anymore.

I was only living in Tennessee for one year, and I bought a house. I was doing very well down there. I was for sure making more money than I had ever made before. Everything happened so quickly for me down there. I felt like everything was great from the start.

I needed to meet new people down there, so I got involved with a strange kind of service to meet new people. It was a phone service. You make a recording, and other people can hear you, and they can respond. I seriously had no idea how it worked, but I did it. I received a response from someone one day, but it was very difficult to understand her. She had a serious accent, and I couldn't even understand her name at first. I agreed to meet her, but it was strange going to meet someone when I had no idea what she looked like.

We agreed to meet at a public place, so we met at McDonald's. I got there first, and I sat and waited. I saw someone come in, she went straight to the restroom, then she went back outside to her car. I had a feeling that was her, so I followed her outside. I said, I am Jason, are you here to meet me? She said, yes, but I wasn't sure if that was you. She said, "I am Deanna. I guess it worked out okay that way. If I didn't like the way she looked, I didn't have to follow her outside. She was attractive though. So, that is how I met Deanna.

Things were going well for a while, so she moved in with me. Everything continued going very well, so we got married on November 21st, 2005.

After we got married, she changed. It didn't make any sense to me, but it got bad quickly. By February 2006, I asked her to leave my house. I wasn't going to put up with dumb bullshit. Deanna was so jealous of my friend Jamie even though she lived four hundred and sixty miles away. Deanna only met my friend twice, but she always made comments about her, and it caused many problems.

My younger brother introduced me to MySpace around that time, and I thought it was cool to be able to reconnect with friends I haven't seen in many years. Deanna started accusing me of looking for other girls on there. It was just unnecessary drama with her. I just didn't need it during that time.

She came back a couple of times, but it still didn't work out. It was always the same accusations. Every time I told her to leave, she didn't waste any time hooking up with someone new. I remember one of those times, it was the very same day. I didn't get that. She was with me so when did she have time to meet someone new so quickly. That is the way it usually goes, the one doing the accusing, is the one actually doing it.

I didn't really know anyone down in Tennessee yet. I didn't even know who to screw around with even if I wanted too. It didn't last very long. There really isn't much to say about Deanna. I got a second divorce in 2006.

Something very cool to me is, the Steelers went to the Super Bowl in the same year when I got married the first two times.

By 2011, my family had all gone their separate ways. After everything that had happened, I didn't care what any of them were doing. I just knew what I had to do. The kids and I were doing okay during that time. I was working at a different job and raising my two kids on my own. Actually, I liked it that way.

In September of 2011, I went out with some friends from work. I didn't drink much while I was living in Tennessee, but I went out a few times to drink. While I was out that night, I noticed a girl when I was getting a drink at the bar, and we kind of made eye contact, but I went on my way after I got my drink.

A little later in the night, I was telling one of my friends that I should go over and meet that girl. I didn't go right away, but eventually I went over to talk to her.

There was something different I saw in her, but she wasn't what I usually liked. She was very skinny, and I usually liked girls with curves. You know, a bigger chest, and ass.

Finally, I walked over to her, and it was something that I always thought was a special moment. While I was walking towards her, she was walking towards me at the exact same time. I thought that was a good sign. So, I started spending a lot of time with Jessica from that moment on. It was going very well. I knew I saw something that night.

In December of 2011, we decided that we wanted to live together. I moved from my house to hers. She had two kids the same ages as my two kids, and I thought it was going to work out great.

I moved in with Jessica on December 18th, 2011, but by January 1st, it was already a disaster. The whole time I was getting to know her from September to December, she always bragged about being a nurse, but I didn't know it until I moved in with her, she hadn't worked for over a year. I guess she didn't know that there is a difference between being a nurse, and actually working as a nurse.

I also found out some other strange stuff about her. She was always telling me stories about her first husband being abusive to her. She told me stories about her second husband raping her.

She always said that her second marriage wasn't real, it was just on paper for some reason.

Whatever that meant. I just thought, alrighty then. I didn't understand that.

Well, her second husband who she said raped her, was always at her house, and he seriously acted like he was in charge of Jessica, and her kids. It didn't make any sense to me. A normal women would not allow someone who raped her be a part of her life anymore and be best friends with him. I started to see a lot of things were not adding up. Jessica's mom also said that the same guy raped her as well. There was definitely some crazy shit going on.

Jessica had a third husband, and she said that one wasn't real either, it was just on paper. If there was some reason why it had to be done one fine, but to do it another time didn't make any sense to me.

That guy was in the Army, and not around, but he was always calling, and he acted like he was in charge of Jessica also.

I started to realize that she just made-up crazy stories to turn everyone against each other when one of her husband's made a comment about me raping her. I guess she said that same thing about me that she said about her second husband. I was pissed off, and I didn't keep quiet. I confronted everyone about their bullshit. I was not happy that I gave up what I had to move in with her. After I moved in with her, she was acting completely differently. Why in the hell would someone do that, and waste everyone's time?

I was doing everything right as part of a family. Jessica had a very bad habit of diagnosing herself with depression. She never saw a doctor, but she always just diagnosed herself. It was just her excuse to cause problems that weren't really there.

She stayed in bed all day, and it got to the point where she wouldn't talk at all. I know she had plenty to say when I was at work though because my daughter always told me about everything. It was just unnecessary dumb stuff.

Finally, I had enough of it. On March 14th, 2012, I left her, and I moved back to Ohio. I was so glad to be away from her bullshit. Jynelle was the happiest, I believe. Jessica was always bitching about how close me, and Jynelle were. She always said that I treated Jynelle better than the other kids. That wasn't the case. My daughter and I were close, and that wasn't going to change no matter what. Things just didn't come together the way they should have.

Even after I left her, she still kept in contact with me. That didn't make any sense to me. She didn't have anything to say to me while I was there, but she had a lot to say after I left her.

After I left, she lost her vehicle, and she couldn't pay her bills. I was only gone for six weeks, and she wanted me to go back to Tennessee. I guess I was stupid back then, and I should have known better, but I did it. I went back to Tennessee.

Everything was going well when I went back, so we got married on June 8th, 2012. That turned out to be a huge mistake because after we got married, the same bullshit started all over again. This time, she said she was pregnant, and she was acting differently from the hormones. So, she was using the depression excuse again.

When I went back, I found a great job quickly. I was working at Eagle Bend. I operated a robot that welded bumpers for automobiles. I liked that job, and I was working a lot. I was making a lot more money than when I was working construction down there.

I guess I was happy when Jessica said that she was pregnant, but I was also thinking that I didn't want to be connected to her because of a child if she was going to continue acting the way that she had been acting towards me.

After a few months while I was at work, she said that she was taking a bath, and she started bleeding very badly. She told me that she lost the baby. I felt bad over that.

Everything continued going badly. She seriously acted like she was a dictator in the house. One time I even referred to her as Hitler because that is how she treated everyone.

Once again, I couldn't take her bullshit anymore, and I left. It was so bad that I didn't even have anywhere to go, but I left anyway. I packed up our stuff, and we were out of there.

I called a friend of mine that I was working with for any suggestions, and she told me to come to her house, and we could figure something out. I went to Tracy's house for a few days, and I found a house as quickly as I could. I was down, but not out. I did what I knew was best for us. It wasn't easy, but I did it.

The kids and I were doing good when it was just the three of us. I didn't go back to Ohio at that time. I was working at a great job that I didn't want to give up, so we just stayed down there, and I got us settled in our own place.

I didn't talk to Jessica at all anymore after I left that time. I still took it hard though. I guess that is normal even though the situation was crazy. I wasn't okay, but I had to act like I was because I had my kids to worry about. Again, Jynelle was happy to be away from her.

At our new house, Jynelle found a few friends nearby, and I believe that was good for her. I moved on eventually, and I was having fun with a few different women. I was working so much that I didn't have time for much of anything.

In June of 2013, I was on my way to work, and there was a problem with my truck. I was sitting on the side of the road trying to figure it out, and Jessica passed by, and she stopped. She came over to me with a smile on her face, and she was acting friendly. When I noticed her, I said, get the fuck away from me. She just said, oh you know that you love me.

That was the first time I had seen her in a while, and I wish I hadn't seen her that day. Again, I guess I was stupid back then because we started talking a lot again, and eventually I went back to her. I guess I fell for it when she said, our anniversary is coming up, and we should be together on that day. It shouldn't have been a big deal since we weren't together for most of that first year anyway.

I don't know why it mattered to her since she didn't even change her last name when we got married. The reason for that was because if she changed her last name, she couldn't continue getting her benefits, and food stamps. She was so dependent on those benefits, and I wasn't. I went back to her in June of 2013, and it didn't take long before it got crazy again. It went right back to the way it was every other time.

It wasn't going very well around Thanksgiving time, but the day after Thanksgiving, she said, we should start Christmas shopping now. My exact words were, I am not buying anything for you and your kids because you always treat us like we are divided.

Within two days after I said that she was acting like a totally different person. She was all of a sudden happy again, and not saying that she was depressed. It was funny how that worked out, huh?

So, I spent a lot of money on Christmas. I even said to her when it was almost Christmas time, I bet you are going to act completely different after Christmas is over, aren't you? She said, no, but I was right, and that is exactly what happened.

Also, between Thanksgiving and Christmas, she said that she was pregnant again, and we were happy about that. She was acting, and I fell for more of her crap.

After Christmas, she lost the baby while I was at work. I didn't believe her at that time. She was just pretending everything was okay so I would buy her kids Christmas presents. They wouldn't have gotten anything if it wasn't for me. There was no evidence that she was pregnant either time, and she said both times that she lost the baby while I was at work. It was weird that nothing ever happened when I was there to witness it.

I was done with all of her bullshit by that point, and I was just waiting until the right time to leave again. During February of 2014, I remember some other bullshit involving her. She didn't work, but she wanted some money from income tax, so she had someone else claim her kids on their income tax so that she could get money for her kids. That was just more illegal shit from her. That made me sick when I found out about that. That was tax fraud. I don't agree with stuff like that. She did get caught for that though, I think.

As soon as I received my income tax refund that year, I packed up everything, my daughter, and I moved back to Ohio once and for all. I never contacted Jessica again. She did contact me one time to show me that she got the divorce. She wanted to continue keeping in touch, but I did not.

I guess I wasn't very good at marriage. If you add up all three relationships plus the time we were married, I don't think all three of them add up to five years. That is bad, I guess.

Grief is like the ocean, it's deep, it's dark, and it's bigger than all of us.

I wonder how different things would have been if my grandpa hadn't passed away when he did. I have a feeling that my marriage to Heather would have lasted a lot longer than it did. I made a mistake at that time. Maybe I am going to continue paying for that mistake for the rest of my life just because I didn't handle it very well when my grandpa passed away.

Being in a happy, healthy relationship has always been very important to me. I have never had any long-term relationships though. Other than my three marriages, I have just had short-term screwing around relationships. Those were fun sometimes, but that was never what I wanted.

I don't know, maybe after a while, I just learned to not get so attached to anyone so I wouldn't get hurt anymore. I just know that I didn't deserve all of the craziness that I went through.

HOME NOT SO SWEET HOME

The first time I ever drank any alcohol I was at the campground with my friend Darrin. I was fourteen, and I was trying to fit in with other kids that were drinking some beer. I drank four cans of beer I think, and it didn't go very well for me. When I laid down later that night to go to sleep, I got very sick, and I threw up a lot in the tent we were sleeping in. That smell was so bad, and it was difficult to deal with.

I woke up the next morning, and I still felt sick. The mess in the tent from me getting sick was worse than I remembered from the night before. Darrin's parents asked us if we were drinking, but we said no. I said, I just wasn't feeling good. I don't think we fooled them though. I believe they knew. I am sure that they knew the smell of alcohol a lot better than we did. I don't think they liked me too much after that.

It was a couple weeks later, and I was drinking again. This time I was over at my friend Dan's house. I was drinking with him and my friend

Porky. I didn't get sick that time, but it still didn't go very well.

Dan's uncle stopped over, and he caught us drinking. He called Dan's mom because she was working. Dan's mom was a police dispatcher. It didn't take long before the police showed up, and we were charged with underage drinking.

I remember it was kind of amusing when the officer asked us where we got the alcohol, and we told them that we found it on the railroad tracks. I don't think they believed our story since it was summertime, it was hot outside, but the beer was ice cold. I got in extra trouble for underage drinking. Along with getting in trouble by the judge when I went to court, I got beat with a belt by my stepdad at home. I got probation, a fine, and six months suspended on a driver's license that I didn't even have. That suspension didn't really affect me since I didn't even get my license until I was eighteen anyway.

I wasn't doing very well with my drinking experiences at that young age. I didn't continue drinking a lot of alcohol at that time. The next time I believe I drank any alcohol I was eighteen, and one night I was hanging out with my friend Rick Fitch. I was trying to keep up with him drinking one night, but that was a huge mistake. Back then, Rick wasn't someone that you wanted to try and keep up with, or you would definitely pay for it. I know I sure did. I lost count after twenty-two cans of beer, and I got so sick. I seriously thought I was dying from that much alcohol. I felt horrible, but I still made it to school the next day.

In 1995, I was drinking a lot of Jim Beam. I drank half of a bottle one night, and then I decided to drive about ten miles to the campgrounds to see a girl I was dating at the time. I still had a half bottle of Jim Beam in the car with me. The road to the campground was very curvy and winding. When I left the campground that night, I missed my turn. I drove into someone's yard, and I hit a big rock. I guess it was a yard decoration. I hit the huge rock, and I remember just yelling, oh fuck! I just backed up, and I drove away. It did a little damage to my car. That wasn't my finest moment.

I went through times when I drank a lot, and then I went through times when I didn't drink so much. It really wasn't a problem at first, I guess. I wasn't drinking all the time, and I wasn't used to it. I guess that is why I got sick so much when I was younger.

I know I started drinking way too much after the shooting incident happened. I was depressed, and drinking a lot of alcohol is how I was dealing with everything, I guess. I was seriously a mess during that time. In 2002, I was hanging out one night, and I ran into my friend Shane. I hadn't seen him in a while, so we were having fun drinking. I was being smart at first because I walked to the bar that night. After a while, Shane said he wanted to go to a different bar. I said that I would drive us. I walked home, got my car, and I went back to get Shane so we could go somewhere else. I got us there okay, but leaving there didn't go so well. I got pulled over, and I got my first DUI. That definitely wasn't what I needed at that point in my life. I got a few days in jail, a fine, and probation.

I didn't realize it at that time, but that is when I started to notice that one thing leads to another, and then another. Depression led to alcohol; alcohol led to trouble. I wasn't heading down the right road at that time, but I had no idea that was just the beginning.

On March 14th, 2014, I returned home to Ohio again. This time it was for good. I didn't have a plan, or even know where I was going to live, but I packed up my car, and I came back. The only thing I knew was, I wanted to somehow make a huge impact when I returned home.

For a while, I did a good job at that. As soon as I returned home, I got involved in a lot of charity events, and benefits. I didn't even know who the benefits were for, but I was involved, and I did my part to raise money for the causes. At one of the benefits, I even dressed up in a Sponge Bob Square Pants costume to amuse all of the kids that were there. That was a lot of fun, and I was a big hit with the kids.

I also signed up to be a mentor for a little boy. I received the call that I was in fact a part of the mentoring program SMYL on my 40th birthday. That was a great birthday present that year. I was doing a great job at that at first, and it was a lot of fun. I was doing exactly as I planned. I was making an impact.

I was also trying to reconnect with friends I hadn't seen in a long time since I moved away. I immediately started going to the bar a lot, and I saw a lot of people when I was there. It didn't take long before I was drinking way too much. There isn't much to do in Tiffin, Ohio. There isn't much here, but there are a lot of bars in this small town. Drinking alcohol is what a lot of people do here.

The two people I was spending the most time with at first when I came back were Charlotte and Lorie. Lorie because she was one of my favorite people from the past, and Charlotte because we had some contact before I even came back. I already had a plan to see her.

I didn't know Charlotte very well at first, but I knew her, she is very nice. I knew her sister Mandy better. I remember when I was in high school, and I first met Mandy. I thought she was the most beautiful girl I had ever met at that point. When I saw Mandy again for the first time after I came home, I just thought that she was like a fine wine. Mandy just got better with age. She was more beautiful than I remembered.

I spent a lot of time with Charlotte, and it was always a fun time. We went to concerts, and we definitely drank a lot of alcohol. I was personally a mess, but I wasn't letting it show at that time. I was always at my best when I was around Charlotte.

In September of 2014, Charlotte and I were watching a band at the Heritage Festival. It was fun, but I had to leave early to go pick up my daughter from a school dance. Afterwards I went back uptown to spend more time with Charlotte.

First of all, I was late picking up my daughter. I was drinking and having fun, and I just forgot. I felt so bad when I got to the school, and she was the only person left waiting outside. I picked up Jynelle, I took her home, and I immediately went back uptown. As soon as I got back uptown, I went past the police station to go back to the same parking spot I had before I left. A police car pulled out right behind me and turned his lights on. I was going to stop anyway, but I wasn't expecting the police officer to follow me to my parking spot. That night didn't go very well. I got a DUI. I was basically picking up right where I left off when I left Ohio in 2003. Drinking a lot, and now a DUI.

I didn't get any time in jail for that one since I hadn't been in any trouble for so long. I did get a fine, and my license was suspended, but I still kept driving anyway.

That DUI didn't stop me. The very next weekend, I was drinking and driving, and hanging out with Charlotte again. I wasn't okay, but I was doing a good job of pretending that I was.

The last time I saw Charlotte, she told me about something Lorie said to her. It didn't make any sense to me at first, but eventually I figured it out.

There was a time when I was hanging out with someone, and he mentioned Lorie to me. I replied with something like, you can't date her because I love her. After I thought about what Charlotte said, I knew Lorie probably said something to her because she thought that she was getting revenge for what I said to someone.

There was a big difference though. Lorie was being hateful by what she said, and I was looking out for Lorie by what I said. She never knew that though. The truth is, I did always care about Lorie, so I said what I said because I didn't want her to date someone who was known for being abusive to women. I knew that for a fact. I was protecting Lorie.

After that happened, I never talked to either one of them again. I just continued drinking, driving, and hooking up with a lot of different women for a while. I was seriously living my life like Charlie Sheen's character on Two and a half men. It was actually very fun. It all came to a screeching halt on New Years eve.

On New Years eve, 2015, I was hanging out with some friends, having fun. I saw someone, and I confronted her about a lie that she told about me. Of course, she denied it, but I wasn't happy about it. I was kind of a jerk. After that I remembered going outside, and I walked over by my Explorer. I wasn't driving, I wasn't even inside my vehicle, but I got arrested. I didn't understand what was going on, but I was taken to the police station. At the police station I was being even more of a jerk, but I thought I had a very good reason to because I didn't do anything wrong. I was seriously talking trash to the officer. I believe I even told him to put in the report that he was a piece of shit because I didn't do anything to deserve this.

Well, I got my second DUI in three months. The second one was bullshit. I wasn't driving. I wasn't even inside my vehicle. The officer didn't even read me my rights.

I was so drunk when I was arrested, when I was being held in the holding cell overnight, sometime during the night, I couldn't even find the toilet right next to me. So, I pissed all over the floor in the holding cell. That wasn't my finest moment.

I was in jail for the rest of the weekend, and I had video court from jail on Monday morning. During video court, the judge wouldn't listen to me, but I was telling the truth. So, I said to him, if I am telling the truth, and you won't believe me, I guess that makes you the liar. I probably shouldn't have said that. I ended up getting thirty days in jail this time. I am sure the thirty days were because of the dumb stuff that I said.

I should have fought it, but it probably wouldn't have been worth it. During my thirty days in jail, I didn't say a word to anyone, I just sat and thought about how screwed I was by what happened. I lost my job. I was going to have fines to pay. I was going to have to go to drug and alcohol classes. I just knew that I was sinking lower and lower.

I did my thirty days, and afterwards I had to put my life back together. There were times afterwards I heard so many stories about myself about what happened that night.

The most amusing story was that I was fighting the police officer. That obviously wasn't true, or I would have gotten a lot more than thirty days in jail for hitting a cop.

Another story I heard was that I was being a jerk that night. Even to my friends that I was hanging out with that night. I didn't remember that, but I apologized to them after they told me about that. So, I am guessing that I am the reason the cop was there to begin with. I just didn't remember some things. I do remember everything that happened outside though. I guarantee that I wasn't inside of my Explorer.

I was trying to figure out why I couldn't remember certain stuff that night. I never had a problem remembering anything before, even when I was drinking a lot of alcohol. I did notice that when I was in jail, there were times when I felt dizzy, and I was going to pass out.

I didn't drink any alcohol for a couple of months after I got out of jail, but that didn't last. I went back to drinking every day and all the time.

I went through one of the alcohol classes, but I knew that wasn't the real problem. I talked to my probation officer, and I told him I didn't think I needed to go to the next alcohol class. I said, I believe the real problem is my depression. I told him that I needed more help with my depression than I do with alcohol classes. He bought that, so that's what I did. Actually, I just wanted to get out of the alcohol class, but I wasn't planning on taking the therapy seriously. That backfired on me when I missed an appointment and there was a warrant out for me though. So, I had no choice, I had to take it seriously.

2015 was a very bad year for me. I was going through the domino effect again. Depression led to alcohol, alcohol led to trouble, and it eventually led to me losing my daughter. My physical health was getting worse also. I continued having the dizzy feeling, and a lot of times, I passed out and I fell and hurt myself. That was something new to me, and the alcohol made it a lot worse. A lot of times I didn't remember anything when I was out drinking in the evenings.

There were times when I woke up, and I didn't know where I was. I woke up in people's yards, ditched, and strange beds. I woke up sometimes, and I was sore, and my face was busted up. I didn't remember anything sometimes.

When I finally did get home, and get to sleep, it was very difficult to get up and move around the next day. I was never like that before. I had no idea what was going on with me.

I just continued doing what I was doing though. I kept going out every night, and drinking like I always did before. I found myself getting into fights after a while also.

I was always a happy person when I was drinking. Actually, when I was drinking, I was even more friendly, and sometimes more annoying, I guess. I was just happier towards everyone when I was drinking. I did notice that being out all the time, there was also a lot of drama in the bars after a while.

There were times when I was in arguments because people think disrespect is cool, I guess. I wasn't a mean person, but I always stood up for myself. I always confront anyone who has a problem with me.

I always liked to sing karaoke when I was out drinking. I am not always the best singer, and a lot of times I was too drunk to sound decent, but I still sang anyway. I always got the crowd into what I was singing though. I believe I was more of an entertainer than a singer. Sometimes it was just something simple like the way I move my head. Sometimes it was a way I danced around. I always got into it when I was singing. I am a big fan of lead singers who had a lot of charisma. So, I always imagined myself being like Freddie Mercury or Paul Stanley, I guess.

There were a lot of times when I was out, and I met a random woman. I either went home with them, or they came home with me. A lot of times I woke up the next morning, and I had no idea who was lying next to me. There were times when I was out, and I just randomly messaged a woman that I had on social media who I really didn't even know. After I messaged them, they would tell me to come to their house to hook up for the night. A lot of those times, I didn't even really know their names. Most of the time, we never talked to each other again after that night.

I had a lot of one-night stands, and a lot of times I thought to myself, what the hell are you thinking Jay?

I ended up going to the doctor about my getting dizzy and passing out situation. It turned out that I had low blood pressure. Alcohol definitely is the worst thing for that. It makes low blood pressure even lower. I never had a problem remembering anything before when I was drinking, and low blood pressure explains why I started not remembering things.

I was at the doctor, and in the emergency room a lot because of low blood pressure. They couldn't figure it out, but my doctor said that it is usually caused by heart problems. So, I had a heart monitor implanted in my chest. The reports from the monitor always looked okay though. They didn't see anything wrong with my heart in the reports, and the tests. After a while, I started getting aggravated because they couldn't tell me what was wrong with me.

Eventually, I think I figured it out on my own. The dizzy feeling and feeling like I was going to pass out started in 2015. That is when I was very badly depressed. I seriously thought that I was stressing myself too bad, and it was causing me physical health problems along with mental health issues. I just didn't know for sure. I just know it started then, but it got a lot worse since then.

Maybe getting into trouble for alcohol was the best thing for me. I started going to Fireland's because I was court ordered, but if it wasn't court ordered, maybe I never would have gone on my own to get the help that I needed. Maybe getting in trouble for alcohol actually saved my life. I'm not sure if that is accurate, but it really looks that way.

THIS IS GOING TO HURT

On December 21st, 1996, Curtis Esley Williams was born. Earlier that day, I was at my grandpa's funeral, and I said goodbye to my favorite person in the world. Later that same night he was replaced by my new favorite person, my son.

Esley was my grandpa's name, so I knew that it had to be my son's middle name. Curtis wasn't originally supposed to be his first name. Up until the last minute, his name was going to be Jaret.

I planned on naming him after my favorite Nascar driver, Dale Jarrett. I don't know why I changed it. Maybe I changed it because I got tired of it by the time he came, I'm not sure. I ended up naming him after a football player, Curtis Martin. I don't understand why I did that because Curtis Martin didn't even play for the Steelers. He was one of my favorite players from a different team at that time.

I was so happy when Curtis was born. I just wish I was doing a lot better during that time. I didn't quite know it yet, but I wasn't okay after my grandpa was gone.

Curtis went through a lot when he was younger. Curtis was born with fluid on his brain. He was nine months old when he had his first surgery. I was so scared for him. My baby boy had his first surgery to have a shunt put in his head. It had a tube that went down his neck, and into his stomach area.

Everything went okay, but it's not something a parent likes to go through with their child. His first surgery was actually on my birthday in August 1997.

Curtis had ADHD when he was younger. There were times when that wasn't easy to deal with. Sometimes it just seemed like he didn't understand that I was the adult, and he was the child. He didn't like being told what to do.

I was very protective of him though. When he was a month old, I was driving because we had to go to the grocery store. It was wintertime, and the roads were bad. I was driving, and a women pulled out in front of me, and it caused an accident. I turned around to the back seat to make sure Curtis was okay. He was fine. Then I got out of the car, and I yelled at the women for causing the accident and putting Curtis in danger.

One time we were at the go cart track racing go carts. Curtis was stopped and stuck on the track. I saw a guy hit him very hard while he was sitting still. After the race was over, I got in the guy's face, and I was yelling at him for hitting Curtis when he was defenseless. I probably looked like a crazy guy for yelling at someone in front of a lot of people, but I had to defend Curtis.

It was a few weeks after Curtis had his first surgery on his head when his mother and I split up. It wasn't what I wanted, but I guess it had to happen. I didn't like not seeing Curtis every day anymore.

I saw him every chance I could because I was working a crazy twelve-hour shift schedule at that time.

I was young, and I was lost for a while. As time went on, the shooting incident happened in 1999, I didn't get to see Curtis for a while. My ex-wife listened to my family's bullshit, and she didn't let me see him because of what my brother did. That wasn't right. I definitely needed to see my son during that time. I needed the one person who made me the happiest.

I moved to Tennessee in 2003, and I saw Curtis a lot before I left. I thought moving was the right thing for me, but I didn't want to be that far away from Curtis. Everything worked out for the best though.

I was living down in Tennessee for a couple of years when Heather called me and asked me if I wanted custody of Curtis. Heather said she didn't want him in her house anymore because she wasn't going to let him destroy her family.

I said, hell yes, I wanted him. I had no problem taking him. I didn't know why she wanted me to take Curtis so badly, but it didn't take long after I had him before I figured that out. Curtis was a mean and violent kid. I have never witnessed an eight-year-old like that before. It was for sure something new to me. Curtis was never like that around me before.

I tried everything I could when a situation got out of control. It wasn't too bad at first, but it got a lot worse.

As the years went on, Curtis became a teenager, and he was a big boy. Curtis was bigger than I was. He had a big problem with being told what to do when he was in one of his bad moods. One time Curtis was arguing with me, and it got physical, he sucker punched me so hard in the face. It swelled up badly. I couldn't eat right for a couple of weeks. That wasn't fun. I never held anything against him. Each day was a new day. I just tried to talk to him differently, so it didn't appear like I was telling him what to do anymore. That worked sometimes, but not all the time.

Curtis was on medication, and he was seeing a counselor. He even had someone come to our house to work with him. I saw for myself that Curtis was totally different when he talked to different people. I never understood that because I always gave him what he wanted, I always talked to him in a decent way, but I didn't get the same respect that I witnessed him give to some other people.

Curtis was always very quiet when he was doing his own thing. He played video games a lot. To this day, he is still like that.

Curtis always had headaches because of the shunt in his head. It started to get very bad in 2010. So, in February of 2011, we were in the children's hospital in Knoxville while Curtis was going through another surgery. His shunt broke apart because he was getting so big. It needed to be replaced.

I felt so bad for him. He was in so much pain, and there was nothing I could do about it. I stayed in the hospital with for the whole week with him. I only left to go get some good food. We even watched the Super Bowl while Curtis was in the hospital. We were there for something bad, but at least we got to watch the Steelers in the Super Bowl while we were there.

The Steelers played the Packers, and that is the one game I always wanted to see. My grandpa's favorite team was the Packers, and we both always wanted to see our favorite teams play each other in the Super Bowl. My grandpa never got to see it, but I was thinking about him the whole time I was watching it with Curtis. The Steelers lost, but I was okay with that. That was the only time I didn't mind seeing the Steelers lose because it was to the Packers, and I know my grandpa would have been happy about that. The surgery went well, and Curtis felt better after that.

It was later in 2011 when I met Jessica, and when we were living together, I started to understand what Heather was talking about. I had two kids, and so did Jessica. When we were all living together, there were more people for Curtis to be violent with. That didn't go very well. Curtis was the most violent with the two younger kids. A lot of times he was being mean to the younger kids, but it turned to me when I said something to him to protect everyone else.

Curtis was now doing the same thing to me that he was doing at his mother's house. He was now destroying my family. Things were already crazy enough because of Jessica's behavior, but Curtis was making it worse for everyone. I knew I had to figure something out.

I was looking for answers because I didn't know what to do anymore. I had no choice but to get DCS involved. I didn't involve them to betray Curtis, I just thought their involvement could help with more options. The kind of help Curtis needed was very expensive.

Curtis went into a facility for a couple of weeks in Nashville. I thought that was a good idea at that time. I expected the doctors there to get him on the right medication and help him somehow.

That didn't go that way though. Curtis returned home, and it was still the same thing with him. Curtis went to live somewhere else for a while, but he was the same with other people as he was with me. Curtis wasn't doing very good no matter where he was. I kept trying though.

In 2013 we had a court hearing to figure out what was the best thing for Curtis. Everyone there that day was supposed to be on the same side, but it didn't turn out that way. For some reason, everyone was against me. I don't know how that happened, or why I was the bad guy. Actually, I was the only person in the courtroom that day who was telling the truth. I guess no one liked the truth because I was accused of having anger issues myself. It got out of control that day.

Heather knew how difficult it was dealing with Curtis because she went through it before I did. She didn't back me up though. She just said anything to make herself look good, and I look bad.

I probably didn't handle everything with Curtis the right way, but neither did his mom. If I wasn't doing a good job with him, she had the chance to get him back that day, but again, she said she didn't want him in her house. That time she said it in a courtroom. Apparently, it was okay that she said that, but no one thought bad of her.

It was crazy that day in court. It wasn't my fault that Curtis was beating the crap out of everyone in my house. I am sure that Heather doesn't blame herself when Curtis was doing it at her house. Of course not, she doesn't take any responsibility for any of her bullshit.

The only thing I regret about that day in court is that was the last time I saw Curtis for about two years. It hurt not seeing my favorite person for a while. It wasn't my fault the way everything happened, but I wasn't okay with myself because it happened.

Everything was okay between Curtis and I again in 2015. Curtis seemed like a completely different person by then. Maybe he outgrew his anger issues. He seemed to have his anger issues more under control, and it was a lot easier to have a conversation with him. I am glad that he is past that now. We have a good relationship now.

Curtis still has his moments. He called me in November of 2023 from jail because he needed a place to live when he got out. Of course, I said yes. He was in jail for assaulting someone. Curtis got out of jail on December 13th, 2023, and he has been living with me since then. He has been doing good since he has been here. He is still kind of quiet and plays his video games. I tried to get him interested in writing and telling his stories, but he isn't interested in much of anything.

Everything was going good until March 1st. I told Curtis before he moved in with me that he has to follow my rules. I made that clear because I remember how bad things used to be with him.

On March 1st, I said something to him because he doesn't clean up after himself, and I don't want any rooms in my house to be trashy. After I said something to him, he got in my face, and started screaming at me. I wasn't yelling at him; I just wanted his room cleaned up. Curtis was seriously yelling at me and putting me down. All over a messy bedroom.

I didn't like what he was saying, so I told him to leave. I didn't appreciate him saying that I was never a dad to him. I am the one who was currently helping him though. His mom wouldn't let him live with her. He said some other things that weren't very pleasant also. I told him that I wasn't going to put up with his old ways, and I meant it. He was doing so good, but that all changed over something so dumb. He made it clear that he is still mad about stuff from the past. He doesn't take responsibility for anything he does though. His mom kicked him out of her house when he was a little kid, but I guess he lets her get away with her bullshit, and he doesn't hold anything against her. So, things aren't good again, I guess.

On January 19th, 2000, my baby girl was born, Jynelle Lena Williams. I named both of my kids, and I knew ahead of time that I wanted one of my grandma's names as Jynelle's middle name. So, I chose my grandma Williams. I just didn't know her first name yet. I just knew I wanted something a little different that started with the letter J.

After Jynelle was born, I stayed at the hospital as long as I could that night. When I left the hospital that night, I went to a bar to have a drink, and think of her name. I thought it sounded like a good idea at the time.

A lot of names came to me, but I wasn't sure. I almost decided on Justice, but I am not sure why I didn't go with that name. Now that I think about it, Justice would have been the perfect name for her. Then out of the blue, a friend that I went to high school with popped into my head, Lynelle Rife. I thought that would be a great name, so I changed the L to a J, and I came up with Jynelle. Maybe that was a drunk decision, but it worked out okay. I don't think I ever asked her, but I'm sure she likes her name.

I went back to the hospital the next morning, and I said her name was Jynelle. She was the most beautiful baby of all time. I couldn't put her down.

Well, I did put her down one time that I can remember, and I felt horrible about it. One night when she was only a couple months old, she was being very fussy. I had to get some sleep so I could work in the morning, so I laid her on my chest so we could both sleep. That was working until later in the night I got woken up when she was crying. I dropped her. I woke up, and she wasn't there. Jynelle was lying on the floor crying. I rolled over to pick her up, and I felt so horrible. I was so scared that I hurt her, or I broke her or something. As soon as I picked her up, she was okay, and she stopped crying. Jynelle turned out great, so I know I didn't break my child.

That was a difficult time though. Jynelle's mom and I weren't getting along too well. When Jynelle was born it was only five months after the shooting incident. Once again, something happened around the same time one of my children was born.

We didn't work out as a couple, but I saw Jynelle as much as possible. That changed once her mom started dating someone new. It was someone I knew, and he tried to control the situation, and not allow me to see my daughter. I just think he wanted to believe he was getting the best of me.

It turned into a little bit of a mess. We had a few court hearings about them trying to control how I get to see Jynelle. They tried to tell me I had to be supervised if I wanted to see Jynelle. That was bullshit.

The last time I saw John, I still remember my exact words. I said, I am done with your games. I guaranteed I would get full custody, then I walked away. The next time I saw Jynelle's mom, she was handing her to me for good. The judge wouldn't listen to me telling the truth, but he listened to my lawyer. It wasn't difficult to get custody with a lawyer. Jynelle's mom had three kids by three different men, and she didn't have custody of any of them. Jynelle was four years old, and she was all mine.

Her husband wasn't there in court that time, but he was pissed off when he found out I got Jynelle. Their marriage didn't last much longer after that. That was twenty-four years ago, and that was the last time Jynelle saw her mom. She took off, and never cared about being a part of Jynelle's life. That was her choice, I just knew I had to have my bunny.

I always called Jynelle bunny when she was younger. I don't remember why I started that, but I think it was because it rhymed with honey.

As she got older, I guess she didn't like that anymore. She told me when she was fifteen that she was too old to be called bunny. Jynelle said that it was embarrassing. So, I said, okay, I will call you rabbit then if you aren't a bunny anymore. We both laughed, but she was serious, and she didn't think it was very funny.

It was difficult at first when I got custody of Jynelle. She was a toddler, and it had been a while since I saw her. She wasn't sure who I was at first. It didn't take long before she knew who I was, and we were very close. It was great, I had custody of both of my kids.

I had a lot to learn. Jynelle taught me all about the Disney shows that she liked the best. I watched all of her favorite shows with her, so I knew what was going on. Actually, we taught each other a lot. I had to know about all of her favorite music as time went on also. Some of them I liked, and some not so much. I got her into liking horror movies, and rock bands that were from my time. One of her favorites is Queen, and I think that is cool.

Jynelle got into horror movies. One year she went trick or treating dressed as Ester from the movie Orphan. She looked creepy, but that is what she wanted to be that year. I thought it was cool.

Jynelle loves to read. Her book collection is endless. Reading is something that I was never a big fan of. One time when she was younger, I had to leave and go somewhere. As I was walking out the door, I said to the kids, don't do anything I wouldn't do. Jynelle said, okay, we won't read anything. That was funny even though she was making fun of me because I didn't like to read.

My kids were totally different. A lot of times when Curtis was mad about something, he accused me of liking Jynelle better than him. That wasn't the case. Jynelle always wanted to talk to me about a lot more than Curtis did. She didn't like fighting and arguing like he did. I loved it when it was just the three of us.

When I met Jessica, a lot changed. It seemed like everyone had a problem with Jynelle and I being so close. Everyone said that I showed favoritism towards Jynelle. That wasn't the case. We were always close, and that didn't have to change. It wasn't our fault that no one else in the house wanted everyone to be close. Jynelle hated Jessica because of how bad things were there. Jynelle was so happy when we finally left there. I promised her the third time that I wouldn't make that mistake again, and we would never go back.

Things went downhill when we left Tennessee though. I was not okay when I left, and we returned to Ohio. I was keeping things quiet, and not letting Jynelle know that I wasn't okay. I didn't want her to worry about anything. I always figured things out before, and I knew I would do it again. I didn't have a plan when we left, I just knew I was going back to Ohio. I thought it would be easier to figure things out in Ohio since I would be around a lot of people I knew.

When we got back to Ohio, I didn't even know where I was going to live, but I figured it out quickly. I just knew that that I had to make sure Jynelle was okay and safe. In the first six months we lived in three different places. I started to worry that I wasn't doing a good job at taking care of Jynelle anymore. I still believed that everything was going to be okay.

There was a time in between our moving around that we slept in the car one night. I knew that Jynelle was worried, but I convinced her that everything was going to be okay. That night we stayed in the car, I had to work the next morning, but I knew that wasn't going to work. I couldn't be at work all day, and Jynelle in the car. There was food for her to eat, but she couldn't go all day without using the restroom. So, I couldn't go to work. Worrying about my daughter was more important. I knew I had to figure something out quickly.

Next is when we started staying in the homeless shelter. It was a huge house with a lot of rooms, and other people there as well. I had to do what I had to do at that time. Jynelle was safe while we stayed there.

We only stayed there for one week, and we got a house to live in. We had a house, our clothes, but nothing else at first. I got some help with furniture and other things that we needed so things worked out for a while.

I started a new job after we moved into the new house so we would have some money, but my mind wasn't right during that time. I felt so horrible about myself. I knew that I wasn't doing a good job taking care of Jynelle anymore. I was trying my best, but it wasn't good enough. I knew that I was letting her down, and I didn't like myself very much during that time. I didn't care about messing up for myself, but I hate messing up with Jynelle.

No one during that time knew what I was going through. A lot of people didn't understand mental illness, I guess. They just judge you by the way you are acting, and your mistakes.

It destroyed me when I was betrayed by my neighbor who was also the person who was in charge of the homeless shelter at that time. She basically took over my daughter from me, and I really couldn't do anything about it. I had an empty house, not much food, and no money. I just had to let her have Jynelle because I knew Jynelle was okay and being taken care of. I know I was considered a bad person because of that, but it was the right thing to do if I wasn't able to take care of Jynelle.

After I allowed that to happen, I went next door to see Jynelle, and Jenny told me to stay out of her house. I wasn't welcomed there anymore. I thought she was a friend, and she didn't mind helping me out, but that isn't what happened. She betrayed me, and I couldn't do anything about it because I knew Jynelle was safe with her.

It was bullshit what she did to me, and Jynelle started thinking differently of me also. I don't know exactly what she was thinking because she doesn't talk about it now, but she stopped talking to me for a while.

That is when I was at my worst, and I wanted to give up on my life, and die. I was hospitalized nine more times after that in 2015. I was so depressed, and I didn't have anything left in my life, and now I didn't even have Jynelle.

I don't know exactly how long Jynelle lived with Jenny, but she eventually went to live at my dad's house. I found that interesting after I heard about that because my daughter was living with a guy who never tried to get to know me my whole life. He knew I needed help, but he didn't do a damn thing for me. A year earlier my dad's wife was threatening to take my daughter from me. Well, I guess they got what they wanted. As long as they had Jynelle, they didn't give a shit about me. Then again, he never gave a shit about me any other time either.

I knew Jynelle was being taken care of, but it hurts that I missed parts of her life. That still hurts me.

I was so embarrassed by the way everything happened with Jynelle, and I was destroyed by it. In 2019 when I was doing a lot better, I reached out to Jynelle a couple of times, but she didn't respond to me. I wasn't going to give up, and I reached out to her on her birthday in 2021, to say happy birthday to her. She replied that time. After I said happy birthday to her, I immediately started apologizing to her for everything, but she didn't want to talk about what happened before. We just kind of started over and moved forward. It took a little time, but we were talking a lot more.

In 2021 and 2022 Jynelle was struggling a little bit when she was out of work, and she needed my help. She wasn't sure about asking me, but finally she said that she needed help. I was so glad to help her and do something for her since I missed the past couple of years. I was not going to let her struggle.

My depression got so much better since I had a relationship with Jynelle again. I was feeling better than I have in a long time.

Jynelle and I were talking a lot the past few years, but there were still times when she didn't respond to me. She said that she goes through times when she doesn't talk much. I wasn't sure if I should take that personally or not. It did seem like she talked the most when she needed money.

My mind wasn't right, but I started to think that maybe things weren't really as good between us as I thought they were. Maybe she was getting money from me because she felt like I owed her or something because of my mistakes. Sometimes when she didn't respond, I thought maybe she was getting revenge on me or something. I couldn't help but think that she was only talking to me to get money when she needed help but ignored me when she didn't need help anymore.

Those were my thoughts, but I didn't think I was right. I wasn't expecting anything new to happen while I was in the middle of telling my story, but I found out that I was right. Today is March 8th, 2024. On January 4th, 2024, Jynelle contacted me, and she said that she was still mad about the way things happened in 2015.

I thought that we moved on from the past, but she didn't. Jynelle admitted to me that she got some revenge on me by me giving her money and helping her. I thought that was shitty of her. She would have been screwed without me. If I didn't pay her phone bill for six months, she wouldn't have been able to get called back to work. She wouldn't have had food. She wouldn't have paid other bills.

She said that she was still angry with me because she tried talking to me about a very serious issue in 2015, and I didn't listen to her, and I didn't do anything to get her any help. I have a great memory, but I don't remember what she was talking about. I don't remember her ever bringing up the issue that she brought up. Jynelle was traumatized by a serious issue, and it still haunts her to this day, and I guess I didn't do the right thing.

I wish I could remember the day she was talking about, but I don't. I was in a very bad situation during that time, and I admit that I wasn't taking care of her very good. I know my mind wasn't right. I guess I was worse than I thought if I can't remember something that important. Mental health can do that. It can cause people to forget things. Maybe that is why I don't remember.

Maybe I am a horrible person. Maybe I should have just given up and died in 2015. My daughter has confirmed that she seriously doesn't like me because I let her down worse than I thought. As far as I know right now, we no longer have any kind of a relationship. I don't know if there is anything I can do to fix it now. I have no idea how this is going to affect me this time.

Am I seriously going to get bad again? Am I going to need to be hospitalized again? Am I going to give up, and want to die again?

It has been a month since our conversation, and so far, I am speechless. I noticed that something wasn't right. I also know that I have done a lot to make things right with Jynelle. I thought I did make things right, but I had no clue that she had a secret agenda.

I think I did my part, and the best I could to be a part of Jynelle's life again. She was acting like everything was okay, but now she is saying things aren't good.

I believe I did my part, and it's not my fault of things aren't good anymore. It is her choice if she wants to continue carrying around the hate with her, but I'm not going to do that.

Maybe I am wrong, but I am at peace with everything from the past. I can't let my life get that bad again. I don't like that Jynelle isn't happy with me about something from the past again, but I don't know what to do now. I will continue to try fixing it, and I will continue praying for the best. If it can't be fixed, I wish Jynelle all the best, and I love her so much.

Most men would never admit this, but I will. I made mistakes as a dad, and I wish I could've done a lot better. I feel like shit because I have let my kids down in the past, and I didn't always do things right. I would do anything to be able to go back in time, and do everything right, but I can't do that. I can only do my best moving forward.

I have been through my own trauma throughout my life, and my mind wasn't always right. I don't want to make excuses, but maybe that is the reason I made mistakes as a dad, but I don't know for sure.

I had an appointment just a few days ago with my mental health doctor. I told her everything that was going on with my kids. I told her that I was concerned that I was going to get bad again. I was surprised by what she said to me.

She told me that I need to stop blaming myself. I have been doing everything I can to make things right with my kids. They are the ones who are still living in the past and won't let things go. She also said it wasn't my fault with what happened with my daughter. My mental health was so bad, and it had a lot to do with it. My mind wasn't right, she said. I never thought of it that way. My doctor said, it is definitely not my fault since Jynelle admitted that she was getting revenge on me. I went above and beyond to make things right. Any problems now are their fault. I felt a lot better after my doctor said that.

My kids don't see it that way though. I can't let it get me down right now though. I will just keep trying to do what is right.

GOODBYE MY FRIENDS

I have always been very nice and kind to everyone. Unless I had a damn good reason not to be. I have always just tried to be funny, and make people laugh. I believe I always did a good job of that.

I have always done a lot for the people that I cared about, but I always got treated like shit for it by everyone. It doesn't seem right to me.

I was good friends with Ron when I was in high school. We were different, but we were friends. He always treated me like he was the superstar, and I was just his sidekick. He made me feel like I wasn't good enough when I liked something different than him. A good example of that is, he always had dumb comments when I wore a rock band shirt. I liked country music like he did, but I liked everything else also. That didn't make me a bad person. I also didn't like working on demolition derby cars like he did. I just wasn't into that. That didn't make me wrong when I didn't want to do that when he did. It was just strange sometimes. We hung out a lot, but sometimes I had to take long breaks from him. He had a bad habit of bullying me.

As we got older, I didn't see much of him. in 2006 when I was in town for a few days, I saw him at the bowling alley. I walked over to him, and I told him that I had two extra tickets for the race in Bristol if he and his wife at the time wanted to go. Of course, he said, yes. When the racing season started, he called me, and he said that he needed five tickets to the race. I just listened to him, and I said, okay because I knew how he was.

I hung up the phone, and I never talked to him again. I thought it was so rude of him. I invited him and his wife. He had no right to invite other people, but he did what he has always done. He thought he was better than me, so he thought he was going to get what he wanted. I have no idea how he thought he was going to get five tickets. I had two extra tickets, and that is what I told him in the first place. I wasn't going to give up my tickets to people he invited. I didn't want anything to do with him after that.

I was good friends with Heather and Jeff in high school also. I actually knew Heather for like forty years. I met Jeff when the three of us were working at Burger King in high school. Heather mentioned Jeff to me one day because she liked him, and I encouraged her to date him. They have been together since high school.

I heard about the drama about everything my first ex-wife was saying when I first returned to Ohio in 2014. Heather and Jeff were now friends with my first ex-wife. I ran into Heather a couple of times, and she was friendly at first. The friendliness stopped when my ex-wife was mentioned.

They had been hearing her bullshit side of the story for so long, they wouldn't listen to me, and the truth. There is a lot they don't know. They don't know about the part that makes her look bad, only me. So, my former friends don't like me now because of my ex-wife's drama.

Honestly, I couldn't believe that out of Heather. She betrayed me over some drama bullshit. That is the way it goes though. People will believe the person that they like better, even when it's not the truth. It was stupid shit that got out of control.

In 2002, while I was working at a fry food factory, I became friends with Jamie. I wasn't doing very well at that time, and becoming her friend really helped me. It made me feel better when she wanted to be my friend.

I felt like I owed her a lot because it helped me overcome some of my depression by just being a good friend. I did a lot for her, and her family. We were like best friends for a while. We even kept in touch when I moved to Tennessee, but I did notice that it was me reaching out to keep in touch all the time. Actually, the only time she reached out to me was when she wanted to borrow one of my credit cards when she needed money for something. I was okay with that because I felt like I owed her.

All she did was become my friend. It did mean a lot to me at the time, but she really didn't do anything special. I made a bigger deal out of it than it really was. I really didn't owe her so much.

I guess Jamie was only my friend when I wasn't around. When I returned home, she started acting completely differently. I was a mess when I returned home, and I guess that she followed along with the drama being said about me.

I guess she turned against me as well. Jamie doesn't talk to me at all anymore. I didn't think she was into drama, but I guess she is. A lot of people don't like me for something that isn't true. I just didn't think that she would ever be one of them.

I have no problem telling the truth about myself. So far, I have said a lot about myself, and most of it is embarrassing, and things I thought I would never say. I am doing it though. It is pretty clear that if anyone wants to know anything about me, all they have to do is ask, and I will tell the truth.

I guess people would rather just betray me by what they hear instead of just asking me about the truth. No one ever does that though. That is why there is so much false information that goes around in today's society.

In 2011, I was at work one day. I still remember it was a Wednesday. When I got home from work, I went inside, and my house was trashed. Someone broke into my house and robbed me.

My football and baseball cards were stolen. My DVDs were stolen. My DVD player was stolen. My kids game systems were stolen. Everything that was valuable was stolen. Even a bottle of Jägermeister was stolen out of my freezer. I had no idea who did it for the longest time. I was even at work talking about it after it happened.

I didn't know many people in Tennessee at that time. I only hung out with a couple of people that I worked with. I didn't realize it, but when something like that happens, it is usually someone that you know. It was driving me crazy trying to figure out who did that to me.

I should have known who did it, but I didn't catch it right away. Who else would know to look in my freezer for alcohol unless they already knew it was in there. Only three people knew where I lived, and they all three worked at the same place I did.

I was at work talking about my house being broken into right in front of the person who did it, but I didn't know it.

Finally, I knew who broke into my house when another guy from work told me that Chris tried to sell him some DVDs. That definitely caught my attention. I knew Chris's favorite drink was Jägermeister.

I asked my boss if she could check the records and see if Chris had called into work on that Wednesday when it happened. The records proved that he was not at work that day, and I knew exactly who did it.

That was stupid trying to sell my stuff to someone else at work, and someone I talked to a lot. Chris was an addict, and my valuable football cards were gone in exchange for drugs. Someone I thought was a good friend went to prison for stealing my stuff.

I was friends with Jan for a while. This was unusual because I wasn't close friends with any guys too often. We had some good times hanging out together, but it didn't last very long. Every time I hung out with him, all he talked about was crazy girls that he dated. When he wasn't talking about girls, he was talking badly about all of his other friends. That was so annoying all the time, but I overlooked it most of the time. Most guys weren't into drama, but he seemed to love it. It didn't take long before he was talking bad about me also. Jan has nice cars, a nice house with a big yard, and I guess that made him think he was better than everyone else. To me that kind of stuff doesn't mean anything if you treat people badly.

Every time I brought a friend around him, he would immediately add them on Facebook even when he didn't know them. Sometimes he even added my good-looking friends even when he never met them. I don't know, maybe he thought that would make him look better or something. After he added them, he would send them messages, and talk badly about me to them. I guess he was trying to make me look bad because I wasn't involved with crazy ugly girls like he was all the time. I seriously think he was jealous of me or something, and that's why he did that.

After I discovered what he was doing, I stopped going around him. Jan still continued sending me messages and saying stupid stuff though. One night I received a shitty message from him while I was lying in the hospital because I was having bad low blood pressure issues. It was just harassing bullshit because I stopped hanging out with him.

After I didn't talk to him at all for a while, I ran into him at a bar one night, and he said, "We need to talk. I said, okay, let's do it. Standing outside right uptown in front of a lot of people, I just unloaded on him. I said, does it make you cool putting your friends down all the time? I said, instead of lying about me, how about you start telling the truth about yourself.

There were two police officers standing nearby, and I said, since you like drama all the time, why don't you tell those two cops about you beating on your girlfriend. That was absolutely true. I was at his house, and I saw him doing it. There have been a few other accusations about him being violent towards his former girlfriends also. The whole time I was saying all of this, he didn't say anything to my face. He just stood there, and he didn't say a word. I guess he didn't know what to say to the truth in front of a lot of people.

I saw him a few other times after that, and he still told me to get ahold of him sometimes. I never have though. He acts like everything should be okay now, but he has never admitted his bullshit. I have no use for anyone like that. I don't need him. I was always a good friend to him, but he was nothing but drama. I should have known better to be friends with him in the first place since he was friends with my sister.

In 2017, I was hanging out in a bar one night, and I saw the two most beautiful women I have ever seen. I went over to them, and I met Cindy and Sarah. They were twins. From that moment I met them we became instantly good friends. We hung out a lot, usually drinking, and going to watch bands play when they came to town. I always done a lot for them both. I always liked to pay for things when we hung out together. I just always liked to do as much as possible for them. I always enjoyed spending my time with them both. Spending time with them is when I was the happiest.

After a while of just meeting in bars, and drinking, I started reaching out to them more personally. That is how I treat friends that mean a lot to me. I wasn't okay during that time, but I never let them know it. I was always at my best when I was around them both. They were my favorite friends, so I tried being closer to them. I always felt like I was more valuable just by being around them.

I felt so bad when someone got Sarah pregnant and then abandoned her. So, I stepped up to help her. I bought her a lot of nice stuff for her baby.

Looking back on it now, I probably should have saved my money since she let the asshole off the hook and didn't even report him to child support. I thought that I was doing the right thing for Sarah though.

I can't believe anyone would treat her like that. Sarah is so perfect. She is truly an angel. I remember one night when the three of us were hanging out, and they told me about him, and he had a girlfriend. I was not happy about that, and I said something to him when he showed up.

Sarah is better than that. Only a piece of shit person would use her like that. I guess I was right because he got her pregnant, and then abandoned her. Sarah let him get away with it though.

I started to notice that the more I personally reached out to them to make plans to do something, I was being ignored a lot more. One night when we were hanging out, I mentioned being ignored to Cindy. She just said that she isn't on messenger very much. I instantly knew that was an accuse, and a lie.

It was an instant messenger, so you don't have to be on there, and you will still receive the message. I didn't say anything, but I knew I was being ignored.

I started to realize that I was being a good friend to them, but they didn't really consider me anything. We talked about making plans to go out of town one weekend, but when the time came, I contacted Cindy, and I was ignored again. I had a feeling that I was going to be ignored so I was prepared. I sent her another text message, and I said, I just thought we were good friends, but I guess not. Thanks for ignoring me all the time.

I guess my text message was correct because she didn't respond to that one either. We never talked again.

The last thing Sarah said to me was that I cared too much. Caring about people is the right way to be, and that is the way I was. She said that like caring about people is a bad thing. I didn't understand that.

The truth is, I did start to care a lot more about Sarah. I thought that she was the most beautiful, sexy, sweet, kind, perfect, amazing women I knew. She was so wonderful. I had a good feeling about Sarah. I truly believe that she could change the world someday, and she didn't even know it.

Being betrayed by them both really breaks my heart. I know that I did everything I could to be a great friend to them both. I miss them both, and I wish them the best.

I was dating Shelly in 2017 and 2018. It was a disaster. I knew she was married, but as far as I knew, they were separated, and it was over. I'm not sure about the whole truth though.

We met at a charity event. I did notice that she seemed like she wasn't there to participate in the games, she was only interested in the bar crawl afterwards. During the bar crawl she came over to me and introduced herself. We hung out together for the rest of the night. We continued dating after that night.

Six weeks after we started dating, I told her I was going to help a friend do some work on his house on a Friday night. While I was busy, she was out with her sister. The whole time I was helping Mitch, my phone was going crazy.

Shelly was calling and texting me the whole time, but I wasn't going to stop working every time to look at my phone.

After I was done helping Mitch, I looked at my phone, and I saw a lot of crazy text messages from her. Shelly was accusing me of being out with another girl screwing around. I was pissed off when I saw the messages. It didn't make any sense at all. When I got home that night, she was at my house. I guess her story changed when she wasn't around anyone else.

I don't know what she was saying to her sister that night, but it continued the following night. I was out, and I ran into Shelly and her sister, and they started more bullshit.

I overheard Shelly's sister talking trash about me, but she didn't even know that I was standing right behind her. That started an argument because I said something to stand up for myself. I even told her that she wouldn't say stupid shit if she would just lay off the drugs. Shelly could have put an end to all the drama by just telling the truth.

Now, I had unnecessary drama from her sister, and her sister's friend. Her sister's friend was actually my cousin, but I guess he loves drama, and lying bullshit. He continued it though because one time I had to confront him, and let him know, if his drama continues, I will put an end to him. It was just dumb stuff.

I gave Shelly another chance, but it didn't go any better. One night when we were out, she told me to buy her a drink. I said, I didn't have much cash on me. She said, if I didn't buy her drinks, she would find someone else to buy them. I just laughed, and I said, go right ahead.

I was out a lot during that time. Another night when we were out, Shelly was going on and on, bitching all night. I don't know why, but I didn't feel like listening to it, so I walked away. After I walked away, she hooked up with someone else, and went home with him. That was a big mistake because the guy she went home with was the boyfriend of a friend of hers. After her friend found out about that, she was pissed off, and eventually punched Shelly in the face.

I guess I was stupid. I let that slide, and we figured it out. Later in 2018, she did it again. This time I was betrayed by the women I was dating, and a good friend of mine.

In October of 2018, my blood pressure was very low, and most days I couldn't even get out of bed. I didn't go out for about a month because of that.

While I was in bed for that time, Shelly started dating my friend Dean behind my back. Dean even told me that she contacted him, but he thought it wasn't right. He did it anyway. So, he lied to me from the start.

When I was feeling better, and getting out again, I saw Dean. I guess he was just pretending to still be my friend while he was stabbing me in the back.

Finally, I saw them both together, and they came over to me. I said, get the fuck away from me. Actually, I said it two times, but on the third time, I didn't warn him.

I took him down inside the bar, and I punched him in the face a few times. I busted up his face really good. I would have kept going, but his friend pulled me off of him.

I saw Dean one other time after that, but I didn't have anything to say to him when he came over to me. Everyone knows that is one thing that you aren't supposed to do to a friend. I guess they are the only ones who don't know that.

I thought Dean was a good guy before that. I never would have expected anything like that from him. I guess I was wrong. I learned that I can't trust anyone anymore. Maybe it was my own fault because I gave Shelly a lot more chances than she deserved. She was always causing drama and talking bad about me to other people. She never told the truth about me, or about herself. 2018 was the last time I dated anyone. I definitely didn't want to go through anything like that again. I just stayed by myself since then.

This next story involves a lot of people who betrayed me, but the crazy part is, it was for something that I didn't even do. That is the way it goes though; people will betray you even when they don't know what they are talking about. As long as they have a reason to make themselves look good by putting someone else down. Some people just need a lot of attention, I guess.

My blood pressure was so low on April 1st, 2020, I had a mild heart attack. I went to bed that night, and in the middle of the night I woke up because I couldn't breathe. I was very weak, but I was able to get to my phone and call 911. I was in the hospital from April 1st until April 6th.

On April 3rd, someone came to visit me in the hospital, and told me about a lot of slander being said about me on social media. She showed me a picture of two cats that looked similar to mine. A lot of people left comments and were saying bad things about me. I didn't know what was going on, so I told her to say something on Facebook for me.

The first thing I thought of was that maybe my cats ran outside when the ambulance came to get me. So, I told her to say something about my cats getting out. I wasn't sure if that is what happened, so I told her to delete that. That statement was only on Facebook for about five minutes, but I guess people saw it, and I guess it made me look bad. I don't know, but everyone accused me of ditching my cats outside or something.

Someone found two cats playing in a box or something by a dumpster. At least that is what I got from the picture I saw, and what was being said. Everyone accused me of doing that.

It is impossible for me to be in two places at once, and I knew exactly where I was. When I got home from the hospital, I saw my cats were doing just fine at home. They were definitely hungry since I wasn't home for a few days.

It was too late though. I saw everything that was said, and it wasn't good. A lot of people said horrible things about me.

Something that I didn't even do was spreading around quickly within a few days. I even got threatening messages from people that I didn't even know because someone was encouraging more people to spread it around. I got two messages from people that I did know, but I didn't respond to anyone even though those two messages weren't nasty.

Looking back now, I believe I should have responded to Mandy. I believe if I would've told her what really happened, she would've said something to spread the truth around for me. Mandy is great, and I believe she would've done that for me.

All of the comments I saw were crazy. There were people that I didn't have as friends on social media leaving bad comments about me just to be involved in something that they didn't need to be in. They just love drama and putting people down. It was very bad, and I wasn't sure what to do about it.

It didn't surprise me that Lorrie had something to say. She had a bad habit of getting involved in stuff that didn't involve her. She loves saying stupid stuff. She has done it to me multiple times.

Some people didn't really say anything, but they tagged me in their comments to let everyone know that they thought the cats were mine. The crazy thing is, no one that was slandering me sent me a message, and asked me if the cats were mine before they slandered me. Everyone was just guessing and accusing me.

There were two people that had a lot to say that really got to me though. Someone that I didn't even know sent me some screenshots and showed me that it was Amy who was encouraging people to spread around what they thought I did. She was basically encouraging people to spread it around that I was a bad person, and I ditched my cats behind a dumpster in a box.

That really got to me that Amy would do that to me. I have known her for about forty years, and we were good friends. I have done a lot for her, and I guess this is the thanks I get for it. It's not the first time she slandered me on social media. She did it in 2012 for something that I didn't do.

Amy slandered me very badly, and then she blocked me so I couldn't defend myself. I wasn't the bad person; she was for what she was doing to me.

I was friends with her for a long time, and she always puts a lot of drama on her social media every day. She was always putting people down. I guess that made her feel good about herself by doing that. I guess she needed some attention by treating other people badly. It was bullshit doing that to me for something I didn't even do. There was absolutely no evidence that I did anything. I was always good to Amy, but she didn't hesitate to betray me.

It was kind of funny a few months ago when Amy knew that it wasn't true, she sent me an anonymous message, but I knew it was her. She said that she was just concerned for my cats so that is why she did it. I just laughed because that was bullshit. If she was really concerned, she would have asked me about my cats, and she wouldn't have slandered me. None of what she said made any sense because they weren't my cats. Amy knows now that she was wrong, but she still didn't do the right thing, and at least apologize to me. I guess she is okay with her bullshit and being wrong. I guess I never really knew the real her after all these years.

Another person that I was very close to was Shawna. I couldn't believe that she would betray me for something that I didn't do either. I didn't know she was into drama, but I guess I was wrong about her.

We were very close, and it broke my heart when she did that to me. I cared about her a lot. She slandered me a lot and said some very nasty stuff. Shawna is someone else who I have done a lot for in the past.

After I recovered from my heart attack, I took my cats and all of the evidence that it wasn't true into court in front of a judge to declare my innocence. I wanted to be prepared after the threats I received over this. Actually, I thought about suing a lot of people for defamation of character, but I wasn't sure if I wanted to do that. That is probably the only way to make it all go away though. I am still considering it.

After I presented the evidence, and my cats in court, the first thing I did was contact Shawna. I told her that I was found innocent. She didn't respond or do the right thing though. Like I said, that is the way society is these days, no one does the right thing.

It is sickening that a long-time friend would do that to me with no evidence and won't even listen to the truth.

A lot of people will listen to anything Shawna says, and they believe she is a great person, but she proved that she isn't. I saw her a couple of times when I was out, and I told her that she is a fucking liar. She never says anything back. I guess she is okay with her lying bullshit, and she doesn't care about doing a good friend wrong like that.

I was crushed after that happened. I was the most hated person in town for something that I didn't do. I should have been worrying about my physical health at that time since I just had a heart attack, but I had a lot more to worry about. I had sunk very low after that, and I didn't want to go outside at all. I had anxiety very bad. I didn't want anyone to see me for the longest time. I ended up removing all of my friends from social media. I didn't want anything to do with anyone.

After that happened to me, I was at a very low point in my life. For the second time in my life, I considered giving up on my life, and wanting to die. I didn't take it very well that everyone hated me. I thought everyone would be happy if I just died. So, I thought about it.

I did try to get some help from a couple of people to clear my name, but that didn't go very well. I reached out to Danielle because I thought that if she said something on social media for me, a lot of people would listen to her, and that would clear my name. Danielle ignored me though, and I'm not sure why.

I tried to ask Dawn if she would help me. I have known Dawn for forty-five years. When I started talking about it to her, she walked away from me. She wouldn't even listen to me. I didn't even get to the part that I was innocent. I guess she didn't want to listen to me since she is such good friends with Shawna, and she already had her mind made up that it was true. It was bullshit, and it hurt a little that Dawn wouldn't listen to the truth since we were good friends for so long.

I asked Ginny to help me by making a statement for me. We were good friends, and I knew a lot of people would listen and believe her. That didn't go very well either. When I contacted her that night, she started some drama with me. That didn't make any sense to me. She started bitching about something that happened a few years prior when I was talking to her about something because she was a good friend. I didn't know what that was all about, but she started drama with me instead of listening to me and helping me when I needed her as a friend the most. I never talked to her again after that night. Ginny isn't the good friend that I thought she was.

I was always well known for being nice, kind, funny, and always doing a lot for people. Now I was known for being a bad person for something I didn't do. I would never ditch my cats outside. I love animals. I have outside cats in my neighborhood, and I always feed the outside neighborhood cats. I won't let them go hungry. It is insane to think I would do anything bad to any animal.

I was actually on the right path when that happened to me, but I seriously felt like the end was near afterwards. I felt like I didn't have any life left in me. I am so glad that I thought of a good idea that changed that for me.

I don't have any social media anymore. I don't need to be like everyone else and beg for attention like that. I always thought that social media was for connecting with friends, not for trying to destroy people's lives.

I don't have any friends left. I lost a lot of friends over that slander about me. No one has reached out to me in a few years now.

There are a lot of people who know now that it's not true, and I am innocent. It definitely changed my life going through that. I am glad that some people know I am innocent, but no one has ever done the right thing. I just don't understand what is wrong with people in today's society. It is crazy out there.

Being so nice to everyone didn't get me anywhere. It seems like there are no rules in the world anymore. It is crazy when you can't tell the difference between your friends and enemies anymore. It's fine with me if there are no rules anymore. I can play that game if I need to, and I can play it very well.

This might be shitty of me to say, but maybe karma is getting some people back for me. I am sure it is just a coincidence, but a lot of people have died since I started taking better care of myself.

One guy who betrayed me, his wife passed away. Another guy who did me wrong, his girlfriend passed away. A former girlfriend of mine who caused me a lot of pain, her daughter passed away. A former best friend of mine, her daughter passed away. A friend who stole from me passed away. All of these passings happened in the past few years. While I have been healing, and making my life great, some people who have betrayed me have had their lives destroyed by their losses.

I am the one who thought about dying, but I am still standing.

JUST JASON

Well, no one likes me. Everyone I have ever known seems to have a problem with me. My kids aren't happy with me. My family never cared about me. Every story has a villain, and maybe I am the villain in my own story. I don't believe so, but maybe I am. It kind of looks that way. Right?

I seriously wish I had some good stories to talk about, but I really don't. My life has been nothing but pain. I can still hear the voices in my head. I can still feel all of the pain in my heart. I had to keep believing that things would be okay.

I have always been just an average person. So, let me take a few minutes to tell you a little bit about me.

My interests have always been music, movies, sports, and just simple things. I am into a lot more, but those are the hot topics.

My favorite sports teams are the Pittsburgh Steelers, Boston Celtics, New York Yankees,

Ohio State Buckeyes, and the Boston Bruins. I love all of my favorite teams. I have seen them all go through good years, and the bad. Not a lot of people can say this, but I have seen all of my teams win a Championship.

It's not easy living in Ohio and being a Steelers fan. Even though the Steelers have dominated the Browns for the past twenty-three years, the Browns fans talk so much trash. It gets crazy sometimes. Up until the last couple of years, trash is what the Browns have been as a team. Maybe Browns fans say dumb stuff because they are jealous or something because the Steelers have beaten them so much for so long. It is very annoying sometimes.

I don't talk trash about sports. I like to talk about the facts. What is the point of saying stupid stuff if your team can't back you up?

I was very young when music became a big part of my life. The Beatles, Queen, and Kiss were the first bands I liked, and they still are my favorites.

The 1980's was a cool time for music to me. Motley Crue and L.A. Guns were my favorites from that decade. I still like them both.

The 1990's were different to me. A lot of the bands I liked were fading away during that time, and I couldn't get into 90's music. There were a couple bands I liked, but I couldn't get into most of the music during that time.

Some of my favorites since the 90's are, Rev Theory, Sixx A.M., Buckcherry, and Rob Zombie.

I like so much different kinds of music. I guess it just depends on my mood. I even like country music. I got into country music in 1986 when I first saw Dwight Yoakam. I thought he sounded different, and he dressed cool. It was different to me, and I really got into liking him. Dwight Yoakam has always been my favorite country music singer.

I also became big fans of George Straight and John Michael Montgomery. None of them do a lot anymore, but they are still my all-time favorites. I don't get into any new country music.

I have been into watching movies since I was very young. My favorites have always been horror movies. One of the first movies I can remember watching is Helter Skelter. The movie about Charles Manson. After seeing that, I immediately became a fan of his. I got interested in the true story, and the facts.

There have been times when I was out in public, and I brought up something about Charlie. People thought that it was strange because I knew so much about him.

Well, I think it's better to know the facts instead of saying something that isn't true about someone no matter who it is.

I really like true crime documentaries. I like to know the true stories about serial killers, and murderers. True crime stories are very popular. I find it interesting that they won't just let them fade away. They make so many new movies about serial killers instead of letting them be forgotten. Most of them are still being talked about today when they don't even matter anymore. Why do they keep them relevant?

When I was younger, I never really liked action movies. I have seen some, but I didn't get into them until the year 2000. It was twelve years after it came out, but I decided to give Die Hard a chance, and I loved it. After that, I went out and bought all of Bruce Willis's movies. They are all good.

I can sit and watch movies for hours at a time. I go to the theatre a lot, and I see every movie that comes out that I feel I need to see.

Helter Skelter is my favorite movie probably. My current favorite movies are, Joker, Bohemian Rhapsody, Atomic Blonde, Peppermint, X, Pearl, and Red Sparrow.

I am looking forward to Joker 2, and Maxxxine that are coming out later this year.

I find the Joker movie interesting because I really relate to the Joker. He just wanted to be a comedian and be funny, but he got overlooked, and kicked around for it. I felt that same way most of the time. I just pray that I never completely turn to the dark side like the Joker did though.

I do go through times when I just can't concentrate because my thoughts are running wild. I can't get into watching anything when that is happening. I am still working on that.

I always like to do good things for people. I truly enjoy being kind to everyone. I know it doesn't sound like it from some of the stories I have told you, but I am very nice, and I do a lot of good things.

I have stayed in the homeless shelter before, so I know what it's like there. I like to donate food to the homeless shelter as often as I can.

I have been a volunteer at the humane society since 2017. I love going there and taking the dogs outside to play and run around. I enjoy that. Every time I am there, I want to take some dogs home with me. They have new dogs all the time. I have always liked dogs more, but I love cats also. I love all animals. Spending time with the cats and dogs is good for my mental health.

I like to keep to myself most of the time now. I don't get into a lot of drama, but I seem to be involved in a lot of it. It isn't because of me though. I am not the kind of person who sits around and talks badly about people all the time. I don't judge anyone.

It says in the Bible that no one has the power to judge anyone. That saying, only God can judge me isn't something that Tupac made up to come up with a hit song. He stole it from the Bible. I wonder how many people that say that, or get it tattooed on them actually know that. I remember a while back; everyone was saying that because of a popular song.

I have been around people who talk trash about celebrities because of something they have done. Yeah, I don't do that either if I don't know the facts. I don't get why people would put down millionaires. They obviously aren't any better than they are. The only thing they are proving is what kind of person they really are.

Times have really changed. In the 1970's, John Lennon was singing, Give Peace a Chance, in the 1990's, Tupac was singing, Fuck the World. Music influences people. A lot of things changed in the 1990's. The one thing that I don't agree with is, disrespect became cool during that time. Disrespect is so common these days, and people don't even realize they are doing it, I don't think. A lot of today's slang is disrespectful. Hip Hop and Rap music became very popular in the 1990's, and apparently it became cool to call women bitches and hos. Well, I don't agree with that. I have been out, and people I didn't know called me the N word. I don't agree with using that word no matter who you are referring to. I don't talk like that, and I don't appreciate it when someone talks to me like that.

Another good example of something that changed in the 1990's is wrestling. The wrestling business was very low in the early 90's. In the 1980's people loved the good guys, and they hated the bad guys. I guess people got tired of hearing Hulk Hogan say, say your prayers, and take your vitamins. That changed again in 1996. Hulk Hogan became a bad guy, and it became cool again. On the other wrestling channel, DX was pointing to their crotch and saying, suck it. Steve Austin was drinking beer, raising hell, and being an anti-authority. People loved it when wrestling became more disrespectful. The ratings were off the charts during that time. I admit, I enjoyed it a lot more when it changed. It was just a TV show. It wasn't real life that I was endorsing.

This next example I have heard of, but I didn't know all of the facts until recently when I watched the documentary. It really caught my attention. Barney was a purple dinosaur that children loved. Barney was a good show for children to watch. I guess people had a problem with a show that was good for their children. Parents hated Barney. I used to watch that show with my children, and I admit it was annoying. I wouldn't destroy a guy that was good for my children though. The rumors started about the guy that played Barney. People seriously destroyed that guy. I find it very disturbing that people would destroy a guy for no reason.

In the area where I live, a lot of young people are dying from overdoses. None of them are older people, they are people that were born in the 1990's. It is sad that that is the lifestyle people are being born into now. I am not a big fan of things from the 1990's. It doesn't seem very positive to me. I am sure there are a lot more examples I could use, but those are the ones that come to mind. I am sure if you really think about it, you can think of a lot more things that changed during that time that isn't for the better.

I don't have any social media anymore because of that. I love my cats, and I always shared pictures of them on social media. Somehow, everyone turned that into a bad thing. It is very disturbing how disrespectful people are to do something like that with no evidence. It was just hateful people who apparently needed some attention by putting me down. I guess their lives are so boring that they felt like they had to destroy mine.

Okay, I got a little off topic, but I have been very bitter and angry for a while because of that.

I am sure something similar has happened to a lot of people. Disrespect is not okay though. A lot of people like to say, let's make America great again. Well, it shouldn't have anything to do with who the president is. America can be great again if people start treating each other better. That would be a good start.

If people don't think the things they say can affect people, they are wrong. John Lennon might still be alive today if it wasn't for something that he said. Mark David Chapman was a huge Beatles fan, but after John Lennon said that the Beatles were more famous than Jesus, that affected Mark Chapman, and he shot John Lennon.

If a reporter didn't say in an article that Karen Carpenter was chubby, she might not have wanted to lose so much weight, and she might still be here today. If that comment was not printed about her, we could have gotten a lot more great music from the Carpenters.

I am sure a lot of people have something about themselves that they don't like. I have always hated it that I am too thin. I have tried to gain weight for years, but I never could. I used to work out, but I never saw any results, so I gave it up. I think that is why I started getting so many tattoos. I figured if I was covered in tattoos, then people would notice them, and not how thin I am. I ended up getting a lot of tattoos that I don't really care for now, but I guess I am stuck with them now.

My dreams are something else that bothers me sometimes. My dreams seem so real sometimes.

I have been through a lot in my life, and I still have dreams about a lot of my life. Sometimes I seriously can't tell if it's real or not. I know they are just dreams, but it is like I am reliving sad parts of my life all over again. My dreams aren't very pleasant sometimes.

I have a very bad habit of repeating myself a lot. I know I did it while I was telling this story, but a lot of stories really did go together so I had to say some things again. I also repeat myself when I talk. I don't know why I do it, but sometimes I say the same thing right after I just said it. I don't know, maybe I didn't get the response I was looking for the first time. I don't know if anyone else notices it when I talk, but I always catch myself doing it.

I don't like being in water. I love being around water. I love being out on a boat. I love fishing. I just don't like being in water itself. I don't know why, but I think I just don't like being in water when I can't see the bottom. I believe I just don't like the feeling of possibly getting stuck in water by the unknown. That is just a feeling that I am not comfortable with. I am fine as long as I can see the bottom of whatever I am in that contains water.

I also like conspiracy theories. I like things that make me think about other possibilities. My favorite conspiracy theory is, did Paul McCartney really die in 1966, and was he really replaced by a lookalike named William Campbell? If it's not true, they sure left a lot of clues about it in songs and album covers. I read every article I have seen about it, and I have watched every video I see because I want to find the one clue that will reveal the truth.

Another conspiracy theory I like is, did the Titanic really sink? Or was it the Olympic? Did they really switch the two ships, and commit insurance fraud? If that is really true, it is sad because they knew there was a chance, they weren't going to make it, and all those people were going to die. This one may never be solved because they are probably never going to bring the Titanic up. It really makes me think though, and I am interested in theories like this.

Being in a happy, healthy relationship has always been important to me. I guess I am not good at that though. At least not so far. I believe

I have always done my part right, but it still never works out. My best move was to buy someone I was interested in a dozen roses, but that has never worked for me. It was just a waste of seventy dollars like six times. I don't know about this one, but I am not getting any younger.

I honestly believe I deserve better than what I have been through. I have been very bitter and angry for so long, there have been times when I considered getting revenge on some of the people who have done me wrong. I don't know what I would do, but it crossed my mind in the past. I couldn't do it though. I really don't have it in me to stoop down to that level.

It is probably best because I didn't need to get myself into trouble over people who aren't worth it. I remember my thought one time. If I did get into trouble for getting revenge, at least I wouldn't have to worry about a place to live if I was in prison. Yes, I do think crazy sometimes.

I will admit, a lot of things done to me, or said about me, drove me crazy. I go through times when my thoughts get the best of me.

I just want the pain in my heart to go away.
Maybe someday I will get what I deserve.

THE SHOW MUST GO ON

In November of 2019, I moved into a new place by myself. For the first time in a while, I felt like I was going to be okay, and safe. The first thing that I wanted to do after starting over was to get 100% peace in my life and make a lot of things right. I knew I was a mess. I had to make some changes, or I wasn't going to survive much longer.

One of the first things I did was get into attending church. I am Catholic, but I was never involved in church, except when I went with my grandma when I was younger. So, I started going to church three days a week. I didn't like big crowds anymore, so I started going during the week at six thirty in the morning on Monday, Wednesday, and Friday. It has been helping me a lot since I started going to church. It definitely made me feel better about everything. I felt like there was some hope. After a while of going to church, I really felt like I was going to be okay.

I started going to the cemetery a lot more. I have been going there, and just sitting at my grandpa's tomb stone, and talking to him. I like to believe he can hear me when I talk to him. It probably doesn't sound like much, but that makes me feel a lot better.

Another thing that I needed to do was cut down on drinking so much alcohol. My drinking has been out of control for a while, and I knew I needed to change that. It wasn't easy at first, but I did calm down on drinking so much. I know I am feeling better since I made that change.

I started to realize that I don't need to be out drinking all the time to make myself feel relevant. There are plenty of other things I could be doing if that was the case. There was way too much drama being out so much, and that doesn't make anyone relevant anyway.

The next thing I knew I had to do was make things right with my daughter, Jynelle. That was breaking my heart by the way things were between us. That was the most important thing that I needed to do. It took a few attempts, but we were talking again. That made me feel a lot better, and I felt like I was off to a good start. I just didn't see what happened last month coming and find out that things weren't so great like I thought.

I didn't like the person I saw in the mirror every day, so I wrote messages for myself on the bathroom mirror. I wrote things like faith, believe, honest, loyal, alive.

Once I started over by myself, I started isolating myself alone a lot. I just wanted to work on myself for a while. I'm not sure that was a good idea though. Sometimes silence can be very loud.

I was doing a lot of things right for the first time in my life. But being alone so much, a lot of things started popping into my head, and it caused me to think a lot. A lot of those things were things that I didn't want to remember. I wanted to forget about all of the bad things that happened to me in my life. My mind was running wild, and a lot of times I started talking to myself. I was saying things that I should have said back when it actually mattered. I seriously felt like I was going crazy on my own.

Things were running through my mind like, why didn't my dad ever care about me? Why did my stepdad always physically and mentally abuse me? Why didn't any of my relationships ever work out? Why did everyone overlook me like I wasn't someone special? A lot of things like that were getting to me. I guess I never stopped and thought about anything before.

So many things started to clog my mind when I started isolating myself, so I decided to start writing. I was writing about my moods, my day, my depression, being abused, alcohol, and everything else. It was a good idea because I was writing about some things as they were happening to me. I was just writing in a journal.

After a while of writing and telling my stories, I got the idea of writing a book. Actually, I thought about doing that years ago, but I didn't think I could do it. I hated reading and writing anything. Since I was writing in a journal, I got the greatest idea.

Nikki Sixx from the band Motley Crue wrote his first book in the form of a journal. It is called, the Heroin Diaries. So, I thought I could do that, but my stories wouldn't be about being on drugs, it would be about my depression.

I thought it was a great idea, but I still didn't think I would actually do it. I was not motivated most of the time since I was so badly depressed. I kept writing and telling my stories on paper though.

At my next therapy appointment, I told my therapist that I wanted to write a book. He thought it was a good idea. I told him about it, but I still wasn't very motivated about doing it, but he said he would help me any way he could.

I was at home being lazy one night, and I was looking for something to watch on Tubi. While I was looking for something to watch, I came across a show called Scandal made me famous, and I decided to check that out.

I was never a fan of the Kardashian's, but the episode about Kim Kardashian caught my attention. The episode was about Kim Kardashian's sex tape scandal.

After her sex tape was released, she was at a low point in her life, and she wasn't taking it very well. Kim recovered from it, and she decided to turn things around. Kim Kardashian turned a scandal into her empire, and she became a billionaire.

I am sure that I am never going to become a billionaire, but that episode about her made me think, and I decided to do the same thing. I saw that episode after everyone turned against me and slandered me for something I didn't do. Everyone hated me, so I decided that I was going to build my own empire.

So, I got more serious about writing, and I wasn't going to stop until I made my life a success. I wrote every day, and I told my stories.

My therapist got the information that I needed to self-publish books. I wasn't good with computers, but I bought one, and I started copying my writing into a writing format.

In July of 2021, I published my first book called, Living with Depression, Volume 1. I felt so good about myself after doing that. I accomplished something so good that I started to feel great about myself, and my life. I was so proud of myself.

I didn't stop there. in January of 2022, I published my second book called, Living with Depression, Volume 2. After I published my second book, I felt like I was pulling myself out of depression. It felt amazing, and some prayers were being answered. I published a couple of books. My depression was getting better. I seriously felt like I was alive again. It was a great feeling.

Also in 2022, I wrote and published a book called, Psych Ward. It is a true story about me being hospitalized with depression from 2015 when I was very bad. It is a very interesting story. I was writing and publishing all of my stories. I used to be ashamed of my stories, and I never talked about them. I am happy to talk about everything now.

The stories I write about are not easy to talk about and tell the world. The greatest rewards come from the things that scare you the most.

In 2023, I published Living with Depression, Volume 3. I was so bitter when I first started writing, but by the time I got to my third depression journal, I was feeling so much better about myself, so it is a little different. It is still very interesting though. I was heading in the right direction.

I had peace in my life. I got my mind right. I accomplished good things. I felt like a brand new me. Since I felt like a new person, I seriously considered changing my name. I didn't want to be Jason anymore. I thought about becoming Jude. I haven't done that yet, but I am still thinking about it.

It's my life, and I am taking a stand. I am taking back my life, and I am finally in full control of it. I am not going to stop until I feel successful in my life. I promise I am going to prove to everyone that I am a lot better than the drama they bring into my life. The toxic people in my life finally brought out the best in me, and I am kicking life's ass now.

I also created writing journals. I wanted to create something so other people can write stories about their life and publish it someday. I created about sixty writing journals. I made cool covers on them, and they have either 150 or 200 pages with lines for writing. Every cover is different, and some of them, I even put popular names on the covers. I thought it would be a cool idea. I thought it would be cool if someone was on Amazon, and they saw a writing journal with their name on the cover. I made about thirty of them with names on the cover.

I was thinking of anything I could do to build my brand, and my empire. I am going to leave my mark on this world. I also tried writing a couple of mystery thriller books. I'm not sure if I am a great writer when I'm not writing about myself, but I gave it a try.

I wrote a book called Love Hurts. It's a thriller with a lot of twists and turns. I had an idea when I started writing, but as I got going, my mind went off in different directions, and I think that was a good thing because it turned out better than I thought it was going to be. I really enjoyed writing that story.

I wrote a book called Twisted Rose. It is a very dark story about mental illness. That is something I definitely know a lot about. It has a twist halfway through it, and another big one at the end. I believe I did a good job on that one.

Then I wrote a book called Deadly Affair. I think this one is my best. It has an ending the reader will never see coming. I am very happy with all of my books.

I still wasn't done after writing books. I was thinking of more to do. My thinking was, if no one is going to take me seriously, then I am going to accomplish a lot more. The more people doubt me, the more I am going to do.

Next, I started doing YouTube videos. I started telling my stories to the world. I made videos, and I told my stories. I made videos, and I promoted my books. I made videos, and I talked about a lot of things that people can relate to. My videos aren't fancy like a lot of others are on YouTube, but I just wanted to give it a try. You never know what can happen. There have been people earning millions of dollars by being a YouTuber.

I wasn't sure about doing the videos at first because I hate it when I see people leave negative comments on YouTube and social media. I don't want anything negative in my life anymore. I decided to just do it though. I have gotten some stupid comments, but I have gotten a lot more comments with people saying that I inspired them. Inspiring people is what I am aiming to do. If I can go from being as low as I was to doing great things, I want to inspire other people to do the same thing. As long as it is people I don't know.

I don't have anything to say to most of the people that I know anymore. Actually, it has been a few years since I stopped reaching out to everyone. Since I stopped reaching out to people, my phone hasn't rung one time. So, that tells me one thing. All of my friendships were one sided. I don't need anyone like that in my life. I was always good to everyone, but I see now that no one was really my friend.

Another thing I thought about doing was opening a bookstore to sell my books and writing journals. I did go look at a small place that would have been perfect, but I wasn't sure about it. I don't want to take the chance of committing to something that may not work out. Tiffin is a dead town, and I don't think a store selling my books would do very well.

I do know that my books sell good in stores though. My friend Mike down in Tennessee has an antique store, and he bought a lot of my books and writing journals, and he sells them in his store, and they do very well. That works out for both of us. Mike buys my books on Amazon, and I get my money. Then he sells them in his store, and he gets his money back. I have even done a book signing once in my friend Mike's store. That was a lot of fun talking to some of the people who read my books.

I am doing everything possible to get my name out there. I had business cards made, and I pass them out everywhere. Recently I even talked to the Advertiser Tribune and Toledo 11 news about doing stories about me. That should be happening soon.

Another project that I want to do is a big one. I want to make a documentary about my story. I have already recorded a lot of myself telling my stories. That is going to be more difficult than writing books. I have already done some research about it. I may need to get an agent if I want to make a deal with Netflix. They only work with agents. I do know a deal can be done with a streaming service though.

You never know, maybe my books will get into the right hands, and a documentary will be made about me. I love movies, and I think my story would be a very interesting movie. You never see documentaries about people with happy lives. They are usually about people with crazy lives, or serial killers. My story definitely fits into that category. Well, the crazy part, but not the serial killer part.

I am so proud of everything that I am doing. It takes a lot of balls to talk about yourself like I do. A lot of my stories I have never talked about before, and I never thought I would. I am glad that I am doing it. I feel so great about myself since I started doing it.

I am happy right now, and I am never going to give anyone else the power to be able to take my happiness from me. Healing doesn't mean that the damage never existed, it means that I am not going to let the damage control my life anymore.

I wanted to give up on my life in the past, but I am glad that I never did because I am Blessed to be able to tell my story. When I look back on my life, I see a lot of pain, mistakes, and heartache.

Today, when I look in the mirror, I see strength, lessons learned, and pride in myself.

I used to hate not being around a lot of people, now I treasure my time alone. I don't think I would've been able to heal if I didn't do it alone. For a lot of years, I put everyone else ahead of myself, but I am glad that I finally decided to take care of myself. I really didn't have much of a choice. I had to do it.

I learned how strong I really am. A lot of people left me in the darkness throughout my life, and it may have taken me a while, but I finally found out that I can shine on my own. I wish my grandpa and grandma were still here because I know even if no one else is, they would be so proud of me.

One thing that really helps me now is, I don't care about a lot of stuff anymore. I found out in the past that caring too much hurts me way too often. I never thought that I would stop caring about some people in my life, but I had no choice. I had to stop caring about people who proved that they didn't really care about me.

If people want to continue hating me for something that I didn't do, or because I tell the truth, that is fine with me. I am not into anyone else's drama. That is their problem, not mine.

Honestly, I am okay now, but everything isn't perfect. I still have days when something comes up, and it gets to me. I still have days when I don't want to be out in public because of my anxiety, and I feel paranoid. I feel okay, but depression doesn't completely go away. I am moving full speed ahead now, and I am laying the past to rest.

I have to do the right thing for myself. I forgive everyone who has ever hurt me. I am letting everyone off the hook because I can't worry about them anymore. It would be nice if some people would do the right thing someday. I doubt anyone ever will though. I am not letting anything from the past destroy me anymore. I am better than the drama.

I believe in Jason Williams, and that makes me unstoppable. Since I started writing and publishing my books, and doing great things in my life, my blood pressure has been a lot better. I am not getting dizzy, passing out, or injuring myself anymore. I always wondered if my mental health had something to do with that. I guess I was stressing myself to death, and that was the cause for my physical health issues.

I realized that I don't need to get any revenge on anyone, I am becoming very successful, and that will let everyone know who the better person really is, I believe.

I am in full control of my life now, and no one will ever destroy my peace again. I did a lot to work on myself over the past few years, and since I don't care about a lot anymore, I know I won't respond in a negative way anymore. I have my thoughts under control now.

It's okay if no one likes me, or cares about me, I love myself. I am happy with my life. I am proud of myself. I know that I am an important person now.

I will still do what I can for some people because I wish I had someone like me in my life. I will continue to inspire as many people as I can.

No one can ever hurt me by my mistakes ever again since I am not afraid to admit anything. I always tell the truth, and I'm not hiding anything. I don't need to be in the spotlight, I am shining all by myself from within. I don't know what I ever did to anyone to deserve a lot of things that happened to me in my life, but I didn't deserve any of this. I am just very Blessed that I am still alive to tell you, my story.

If anyone else has very serious mental health issues, please call this number, and immediately get the help that you need.

Mental Health Hotline

567-867-4673

Printed in Great Britain
by Amazon